ON THE
JOB
SERIES

REAL PEOPLE WORKING in

TRANSPORTATION

ON THE JOB SERIES

REAL PEOPLE WORKING in

TRANSPORTATION

Blythe Camenson

VGM Career Horizons
NTC/Contemporary Publishing Group

Library of Congress Cataloging-in-Publication Data

Camenson, Blythe.
    On the job : real people working in transportation / Blythe
Camenson.
        p.   cm. — (On the job series)
    ISBN 0-658-00105-1 (cloth)
    ISBN 0-658-00107-8 (paper)
    1. Transport workers   2. Transportation—Vocational guidance.
    I. Title.   II. Title: Real people working in transportation.   III. Series.
    HD8039.T7C35   1999
    388'.023—dc21   99-25387
                                                            CIP

Cover design by Nick Panos

Published by VGM Career Horizons
A division of NTC/Contemporary Publishing Group, Inc.
4255 West Touhy Avenue, Lincolnwood (Chicago), Illinois 60712-1975 U.S.A.
Printed in the United States of America
International Standard Book Number: 0-658-00105-1 (cloth)
                                                  0-658-00107-8 (paper)
99 00 01 02 03 04 VL 18 17 16 15 14 13 12 11 10 9 8 7 6 5 4 3 2 1

To Denise Betts: Thank-you for our new relationship;
may it be a long and fruitful one.

Contents

Acknowledgments   xi

How to Use This Book   xiii

Introduction to the Field   xv

1. Bus Drivers   1

Overview   1

Training   4

Job Outlook   7

Salaries   8

Related Fields   9

Interview: Heinz Hammer, Transit Operator   9

Interview: Bobbie Ann Zielinski,
    School Bus Driver   12

Interview: Sheryl Kersmarki,
    School Bus Driver   14

For More Information   18

2. Taxi Drivers and Chauffeurs   19

Overview   19

Training   22

Job Outlook   24

Salaries   25

Related Fields   26

Interview: Sarah Benson, Taxi Driver   26

Interview: Timothy Sexton, Taxi Driver   30

Interview: Lawrence Shepard, Chauffeur   33

Interview: Artemio Gonzalez, Jr.,
    Personal Chauffeur   36

For More Information   38

3.	**Truck Drivers**	**39**
	Overview	39
	Training	43
	Job Outlook	46
	Salaries	48
	Related Fields	49
	Interview: Wally Nickerson, Trucker	49
	For More Information	50
4.	**Material-Moving Equipment Operators**	**53**
	Overview	53
	Training	55
	Job Outlook	56
	Salaries	58
	Related Fields	59
	Interview: Terry Goodwin, Overhead Crane Operator	59
	Interview: Andy Jones, Bulldozer Operator	61
	Interview: John Bisig, Operating Engineer	62
	For More Information	65
5.	**Water Transportation Occupations**	**67**
	Overview	67
	Training	69
	Job Outlook	71
	Salaries	73
	Related Fields	73
	Interview: Thomas MacPherson, Chief Engineer	73
	Interview: Richard Turnwald, Cruise Ship Purser	75
	For More Information	78

6.	**Aviation Occupations**	**79**
	Overview	**79**
	Training	**84**
	Job Outlook	**88**
	Salaries	**91**
	Related Fields	**94**
	Interview: Rudy Vanderkrogt, Pilot	94
	Interview: Jim Carr, Pilot	99
	Interview: Gracie Anderson, Flight Attendant	103
	Interview: Karen Seals, Air Traffic Controller	106
	For More Information	**109**
7.	**Rail Transportation Workers**	**113**
	Overview	**113**
	Training	**117**
	Job Outlook	**119**
	Salaries	**120**
	Related Fields	**121**
	Interview: Steve Nichols, Terminal Superintendent	122
	For More Information	**126**
8.	**Travel Agents**	**127**
	Overview	**127**
	Training	**128**
	Job Outlook	**129**
	Salaries	**130**
	Related Fields	**131**
	Interview: Vivian Portela Buscher, Travel Agent	131
	Interview: Mary Fallon Miller, Travel Agent	133
	For More Information	**135**
	About the Author	**137**

Acknowledgments

The author would like to thank the following professionals for providing information about their careers:

- Gracie Anderson, flight attendant

- Sarah Benson, taxi driver

- John Bisig, operating engineer

- Vivian Portela Buscher, travel agent

- Jim Carr, pilot

- Artemio Gonzalez, Jr., personal chauffeur

- Terry Goodwin, overhead crane operator

- Heinz Hammer, transit operator

- Andy Jones, bulldozer operator

- Sheryl Kersmarki, school bus driver

- Thomas MacPherson, chief engineer

- Mary Fallon Miller, travel agent

- Steve Nichols, terminal superintendent

- Wally Nickerson, trucker

- Karen Seals, air traffic controller

- Timothy Sexton, taxi driver

- Lawrence Shepard, chauffeur

- Richard Turnwald, cruise ship purser

- Rudy Vanderkrogt, pilot

- Bobbie Ann Zielinski, school bus driver

How to Use This Book

On the Job: Real People Working in Transportation is part of a series of career books designed to help you find essential information quickly and easily. Unlike other career resources on the market, books in the *On the Job* series provide you with information on hundreds of careers, in an easy-to-use format. This includes information on:

- Nature of the work

- Working conditions

- Employment

- Training, other qualifications, and advancement

- Job outlooks

- Earnings

- Related occupations

- Sources of additional information

But that's not all. You'll also benefit from a first-hand look at what jobs are really like, as told in the words of the employees themselves. Throughout the book, one-on-one interviews, with dozens of practicing professionals, enrich the text and enhance your understanding of life on the job.

These interviews tell what each job entails, what the duties are, what the lifestyle is like, and what the upsides and downsides are. All of the professionals reveal what drew them to the field and how they got started. And to help you make the best career choice for yourself, each professional offers you some expert advice based on years of personal experience.

Each chapter also lets you see at a glance, with easy-to-use reference symbols, the level of education required and salary range for the featured occupations.

So, how do you use this book? Easy. You don't need to run to the library and bury yourself in cumbersome documents from the Bureau of Labor Statistics, nor do you need to rush out and buy a lot of bulky books you'll never look at. All you have to do is glance through our extensive table of contents, find the fields that interest you, and read what the experts have to say.

Introduction to the Field

The transportation industry is one of the largest employers in North America. If you're reading this book, chances are you're already considering a career in this fast-growing profession.

Glancing through the table of contents will give you an idea of all the choices open to you. But perhaps you're not sure of the working conditions the different transportation areas offer or which area would suit your personality, skills, and lifestyle the most. There are several factors to consider when deciding which sector of the transportation industry to pursue. Each field carries with it different levels of responsibility and commitment. To identify occupations that will match your expectations, you need to know what each job entails.

Ask yourself the following questions and make note of your answers. Then, as you go through the following chapters, compare your requirements to the information provided by the professionals interviewed. Their comments will help you pinpoint the fields that would interest you, and eliminate those that would clearly be the wrong choice.

- How much time are you willing to commit to training? Some skills can be learned on-the-job; others can take much longer and require a year or two or more of formal training.

- How much people contact do you want your job to have? Some jobs, such as long-distance truck driving, offer few opportunities for day-to-day contact; other positions, such as travel agent or flight attendant, depend on people contact to be successful.

- How much time away from home are you willing to spend? Some transportation jobs will have you away from your family on a regular basis.

- How much money do you expect to earn starting out and after you have a few years' experience under your belt? In general, those areas that pay the most also require the largest investment of time for training.

- Will the actual work offer enough of a challenge? Will it provide you with a sense of accomplishment, or will it become tedious after you've learned the ropes?

- How much independence do you require? Do you want to be your own boss or will you be content as a salaried employee?

- Will you work normal hours? Or will your day start at 5:30 A.M. and not end until thirteen or fourteen hours later? Can you handle working weekends and holidays?

- How much stress can you handle? Would you prefer to avoid work that could be emotionally draining?

Knowing what your expectations are and then comparing them to the realities of the work will help you make informed choices.

Although *On the Job: Real People Working in Transportation* strives to be as comprehensive as possible, not all jobs in this extensive field have been covered or given the same amount of emphasis. If you still have questions after reading this book, there are a number of other avenues to pursue. You can find out more information by contacting the sources listed at the end of each chapter. You can also find professionals on your own to talk to and observe as they go about their work. Any remaining gaps you discover can be filled by referring to the *Occupational Outlook Handbook*.

REAL PEOPLE WORKING in

TRANSPORTATION

CHAPTER 1 Bus Drivers

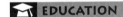

EDUCATION
H.S. preferred

$$$ SALARY/EARNINGS
$25,000 to $35,000

OVERVIEW

Bus drivers provide transportation for millions of Americans every day. Intercity bus drivers transport people between regions of a state or of the country; local transit bus drivers, within a metropolitan area or county; motorcoach drivers, on charter excursions and tours; and school bus drivers, to and from schools and related events.

All drivers follow time schedules and routes over highways and city and suburban streets to provide passengers with an alternative to the automobile and other forms of transportation.

Intercity bus drivers and local transit bus drivers report to their assigned terminals or garages, where they receive tickets or transfers and prepare trip report forms.

School bus drivers do not always have to report to an assigned terminal or garage. In some cases, school bus drivers often have the choice of taking their bus home, or parking it in a more convenient area.

Before beginning their routes, drivers check their vehicle's tires, brakes, windshield wipers, lights, oil, fuel, and water supply. Drivers also verify that the bus has safety equipment, such as fire extinguishers, first aid kits, and emergency reflectors.

Drivers pick up and drop off passengers at bus stops, stations, or, in the case of students, at regularly scheduled neighborhood locations.

Intercity and local transit bus drivers collect fares; answer questions about schedules, routes, and transfer points; and sometimes announce stops.

School bus drivers do not collect fares. Instead, they prepare weekly reports with the number of students, trips or runs, work hours, miles, and the amount of fuel consumption. Their supervisors set time schedules and routes for the day or week. School bus drivers also must maintain order on their bus and enforce school safety standards by allowing only students to board.

Bus drivers' days are run by the clock, as they must adhere to strict time schedules. Drivers must operate vehicles safely, especially when traffic is heavier than normal. However, they cannot let light traffic put them ahead of schedule so that they miss passengers.

Bus drivers must be alert to prevent accidents, especially in heavy traffic or in bad weather, and to avoid sudden stops or swerves that jar passengers.

School bus drivers must exercise particular caution when children are getting on or off the bus. They must know and reinforce the same set of rules used elsewhere in the school system.

Bus routes vary. Local transit bus drivers may make several trips each day over the same city and suburban streets, stopping as frequently as every few blocks.

School bus drivers also drive the same routes each day, stopping to pick up pupils in the morning and return them to their homes in the afternoon. School bus drivers may also transport students and teachers on field trips or to sporting events.

Intercity bus drivers may make only a single one-way trip to a distant city or a round trip each day, stopping at towns just a few miles apart or only at large cities hundreds of miles apart.

Motorcoach drivers transport passengers on charter trips and sightseeing tours. Drivers routinely interact with customers and tour guides to make the trip as comfortable and informative as possible. They are directly responsible for keeping to strict schedules, adhering to the guidelines of the tours' itinerary, and the overall success of the trip. Trips frequently last more than one day, and if they are assigned to an extended tour, they may be away for a week or more.

Local transit bus drivers submit daily trip reports with a record of tickets and fares received, trips made, and significant delays in schedule. They also report mechanical problems. All bus drivers must be able to fill out accident reports when necessary.

Intercity drivers who drive across state or national boundaries must comply with U.S. Department of Transportation regulations. These include completing vehicle inspection reports and recording distances traveled and the periods of time they spend driving or off duty and performing other duties.

Driving a bus through heavy traffic while dealing with passengers is not physically strenuous, but it can be stressful and fatiguing. On the other hand, many drivers enjoy the opportunity to work without direct supervision, with full responsibility for the bus and passengers.

Intercity bus drivers may work nights, weekends, and holidays and often spend nights away from home, where they stay at hotels at company expense. Senior drivers with regular routes have regular weekly work schedules, but others do not have regular schedules and must be prepared to report for work on short notice. They report for work only when called for a charter assignment or to drive extra buses on a regular route.

Intercity bus travel and charter work tend to be seasonal. From May through August, drivers may work the maximum number of hours per week that regulations allow. During winter, junior drivers may work infrequently, except for busy holiday travel periods, and may be furloughed for periods of time.

School bus drivers work only when school is in session. Many work twenty hours a week or less, driving one or two routes in the morning and afternoon. Drivers taking field or athletic trips or who also have midday kindergarten routes may work more hours a week.

Regular local transit bus drivers usually have a five-day workweek; Saturdays and Sundays are considered regular workdays. Some drivers work evenings and after midnight. To accommodate commuters, many work "split shifts," for example, 6:00 A.M. to 10:00 A.M. and 3:00 P.M. to 7:00 P.M., with time off in between.

Tour and charter bus drivers may work any day and all hours of the day, including weekends and holidays. Their hours are dictated by the charter trips booked and the schedule and the prearranged itinerary of tours. However, like all bus drivers, their weekly hours must be consistent with the Department of Transportation's rules and regulations concerning hours of service. For example, a long-distance driver cannot work more than sixty hours in any seven-day period and drivers must rest eight hours for every ten hours of driving.

TRAINING

Bus driver qualifications and standards are established by state and federal regulations. All drivers must comply with federal regulations and any state regulations that exceed federal requirements. Federal regulations require drivers who operate vehicles designed to transport sixteen or more passengers to hold a commercial driver's license (CDL) from the state in which they live.

To qualify for a commercial driver's license, applicants must pass a written test on rules and regulations and then demonstrate they can operate a bus safely. A national data bank permanently records all driving violations incurred by people who hold commercial licenses. A state may not issue a commercial driver's license to a driver who already has a license suspended or revoked in another state. Trainees must be accompanied by a driver with a CDL until they get their own CDL. Information on how to apply for a commercial driver's license may be obtained from state motor vehicle administrations.

While many states allow those who are eighteen years and older to drive buses within state borders, the U.S. Department of Transportation establishes minimum qualifications for bus drivers engaged in interstate commerce. Federal Motor Carrier Safety Regulations require that drivers must be at least twenty-one years old and pass a physical examination once every two years. The main physical requirements include good hearing, 20/40 vision with or without glasses or corrective lenses, and a seventy-degree field of vision in each eye. Drivers must not be color blind. Drivers must be able to hear a forced whisper in one ear at not less than five feet, with or without a hearing aid. Drivers must have normal use of arms and legs and normal blood pressure. Drivers may not use any controlled substances, unless prescribed by a licensed physician. People with epilepsy or diabetes controlled by insulin are not permitted to be interstate bus drivers. Federal regulations also require employers to test their drivers for alcohol and drug use as a condition of employment, and require periodic random tests while on duty. In addition, a driver must not have been convicted of a felony involving the use of a motor vehicle; a crime involving drugs; driving under the influence of drugs or alcohol; or hit-and-run driving that resulted in injury or death. All drivers must be able to read and speak English well enough to read road signs, prepare reports, and communicate with law enforcement officers and the public. In addition, drivers must take a written examination on the Motor Carrier Safety Regulations of the U.S. Department of Transportation.

Many employers prefer high school graduates and require a written test of ability to follow complex bus schedules. Many intercity and public transit bus companies prefer applicants who are at least twenty-four years of age; some require several years of bus- or truck-driving experience. In some states, school bus drivers must pass a background investigation to uncover any criminal record or history of mental problems.

Because bus drivers deal with passengers, they must be courteous. They need an even temperament and emotional stability because driving in heavy, fast-moving, or stop-and-go traffic and dealing with passengers can be stressful. Drivers must have strong communication skills and be able to coordinate and manage large groups of people.

Most intercity bus companies and local transit systems give driver trainees two to eight weeks of classroom and "behind-the-wheel" instruction. In the classroom, trainees learn U.S. Department of Transportation and company work rules, safety regulations, state and municipal driving regulations, and safe driving practices. They also learn to read schedules, determine fares, keep records, and deal with passengers courteously.

School bus drivers are also required to obtain a commercial driver's license from the state in which they live. Many people who enter school bus driving have never driven any vehicle larger than an automobile. They receive between one and four weeks of driving instruction, plus classroom training on state and local laws, regulations, and policies of operating school buses; safe driving practices; driver-pupil relations; first aid; disabled student special needs; and emergency evacuation procedures. School bus drivers must also be aware of school systems' rules for discipline and conduct for bus drivers and the students they transport.

During training, bus drivers practice driving on set courses. They practice turns and zigzag maneuvers, backing up, and driving in narrow lanes. Then they drive in light traffic and, eventually, on congested highways and city streets. They also make trial runs, without passengers, to improve their driving skills and learn the routes. Local transit trainees memorize and drive each of the runs operating out of their assigned garage. New drivers begin with a "break-in" period. They make regularly scheduled trips with passengers, accompanied by an experienced driver who gives helpful tips, answers questions, and evaluates the new driver's performance.

New intercity and local transit drivers are usually placed on an "extra" list to drive charter runs, extra buses on regular runs, and special runs (for example, during morning and evening rush hours and to sports events). They also substitute for regular drivers who are ill or on vacation. New drivers remain on the extra list, and may work only part-time, perhaps for several years, until they have enough seniority to receive a regular run.

Senior drivers may bid for runs they prefer, such as those with more work hours, lighter traffic, weekends off, or, in the case of intercity bus drivers, higher earnings or fewer workdays per week.

Opportunities for promotion are generally limited. However, experienced drivers may become supervisors or dispatchers, assigning buses to drivers, checking whether drivers are on schedule, rerouting buses to avoid blocked streets or other problems, and dispatching extra vehicles and service crews to scenes of accidents and breakdowns.

In transit agencies with rail systems, drivers may become train operators or station attendants. A few drivers become managers. Promotion in publicly owned bus systems is often by competitive civil service examination.

Some motorcoach drivers purchase their own equipment and go into business for themselves.

JOB OUTLOOK

Bus drivers hold about 592,000 jobs nationwide. More than a third work part-time. Nearly three out of four drivers work for school systems or companies providing school bus services under contract. Most of the remainder work for private and local government transit systems; some also work for intercity and charter bus lines.

People seeking jobs as bus drivers over the 1996–2006 period should encounter good opportunities. Many employers are having difficulty finding qualified candidates to fill vacancies left by departing employees. Opportunities should be best for individuals with good driving records who are willing to start on a part-time or irregular schedule, as well as for those seeking jobs as school bus drivers in metropolitan areas that are growing rapidly. Those seeking higher-paying intercity and public transit bus driver positions may encounter competition.

Employment of bus drivers is expected to increase about as fast as average for all occupations through 2006, primarily to meet the transportation needs of a growing school-age population. Thousands of additional job openings are expected to occur each year because of the need to replace workers who take jobs in other occupations, retire, or leave the occupation for other reasons.

School bus driving jobs should be easiest to acquire because most of these positions are part-time and often have a high turnover rate. The number of school bus drivers is expected to increase as a result of growth in elementary and secondary school enrollments. In addition, as more of the nation's population is concentrated in suburban areas—where students generally ride school buses—and less in the central cities—where transportation is not provided for most pupils—more school bus drivers will be needed.

Employment of local transit and intercity drivers will grow as bus ridership increases. Local and intercity bus travel is expected to increase as the population and labor force grow and incomes rise, but more individual travelers will opt to travel by airplane or automobile rather than by bus. Most growth in intercity drivers will probably be in group charter travel, rather than scheduled intercity bus services. There may continue to be competition for local transit and intercity bus driver jobs in some areas because many of these positions offer relatively high wages and attractive benefits. The most competitive positions will be those offering regular hours and steady driving routes.

Full-time bus drivers are rarely laid off during recessions. However, hours of part-time local transit and intercity bus drivers may be reduced if bus ridership decreases, because fewer extra buses would be needed. Seasonal layoffs are common. Many intercity bus drivers with little seniority, for example, are furloughed during the winter when regular schedule and charter business falls off; school bus drivers seldom work during the summer or school holidays.

SALARIES

Median weekly earnings of bus drivers who worked full-time were $400 in 1996. The middle 50 percent earned between about $293 and $588 a week. The lowest 10 percent earned less than $233 a week, while the highest 10 percent earned more than $760 a week.

According to the American Public Transit Association, in early 1997 local transit bus drivers in metropolitan areas with more than two million inhabitants were paid an average hourly wage rate of $17.06 by companies with over 1,000 employees, and $15.43 by those with fewer than 1,000 employees. In smaller metropolitan areas, they had an average hourly wage rate of $14.04 in areas with between 250,000 and 500,000 residents, and $11.76 in areas with populations below 50,000. Generally, drivers can reach the top rate in three or four years.

According to a survey by the Educational Research Service, the average rate for school bus drivers employed by public school systems was $11.50 an hour during the 1996–97 school year. Lowest hourly rates averaged $9.93, while highest hourly rates averaged $13.06.

The fringe benefits bus drivers receive from their employers vary greatly. Most intercity and local transit bus drivers receive paid health and life insurance, sick leave, and free bus rides on any of the regular routes of their line or system. Drivers who work full-time also get as much as four weeks of vacation annually.

Most local transit bus drivers are also covered by dental insurance and pension plans. School bus drivers receive sick leave, and many are covered by health and life insurance and pension plans. Because they generally do not work when school is not in session, they do not get vacation leave. In a number of states, local transit and school bus drivers who are employed by local governments are covered by a state-wide public employee pension system.

Most intercity and many local transit bus drivers are members of the Amalgamated Transit Union. Local transit bus drivers in New York and several other large cities belong to the Transport Workers Union of America. Some drivers belong to the United Transportation Union and the International Brotherhood of Teamsters.

RELATED FIELDS

Other workers who drive vehicles on highways and city streets are taxi drivers, chauffeurs, and truck drivers. See Chapters 2 and 3 for more information on these fields.

INTERVIEW
Heinz Hammer
Transit Operator

Heinz Hammer has been a bus driver for British Columbia Transit in Vancouver for more than thirty years. He is originally from Germany and has a degree in psychology. He is also the author of *Routes: The Lighter Side of Public Transit.*

How Heinz Hammer Got Started

"I have always enjoyed working with people, always been interested in what makes them tick, and what makes them do the things they do. This interest has always helped me in any situation on a one-to-one basis or working with groups of people.

"I got my job through a friend I knew who worked for BC Transit as a driver. He suggested that I would make a good bus driver. I took his advice, applied, and eventually was hired.

"BC Transit provides an extensive training program, covering how to get used to the size of the vehicle you are operating, the routes, procedures, tips in public relations, learning patience and compassion, spotting cheaters, and recognizing people with genuine needs. The training takes approximately two months."

What the Job's Really Like

"Being a bus driver involves shift work. One has to remember that buses have to be out very early to get even the earliest-starting worker to his job on time. Therefore, driving to work usually happens between 3:00 A.M. and 5:30 A.M., especially for me, since I chose to work the early shift. As a single parent it is important to me to get home early so my boys won't come home to an empty house.

"There are many different shifts: some early, some are mid-runs (usually relieving the early shift and finishing around supper time or later), and there are the so-called 'owls,' which is a shift that starts usually after supper and ends in the wee hours of the morning. It is common for an owl to finish after the first morning runs have already gone out.

"Upon arrival at the depot, you have to sign in. This tells the dispatcher that your particular route is covered. Extra drivers are on hand in case someone sleeps in or books off sick. The runs have to be covered. It is rare that a run has to be canceled due to lack of manpower, but it does happen on occasion.

"Sleeping in as a bus driver is not a trivial occurrence; it is always documented and can result in serious disciplinary action if it happens too frequently. The average driver might sleep in approximately once every year. Some never have.

"After signing in, you find out what particular bus has been assigned to your route. You prepare your transfers, get the bus ready by setting all the signs, doing a thorough pre-check of the bus to make sure all systems are functioning, and you leave the yard about twenty minutes after signing in.

"A paddle clipped to a board tells the driver which routes to follow, what time to leave the different timing points, where connections are made, and any other useful information necessary to complete your day. At the end of your shift it is always nice to see your relief taking over.

"The hardest part of the job is putting up with unruly passengers, uneducated and aggressive drivers, being cut off, or passengers making unreasonable demands, such as: 'Do you go to my Doctor's?', or 'Can you take me home?'

"Most people never appreciate how hard some drivers have to work. After a few years of driving you acquire the following expertise: You have become a chauffeur, baby-sitter, tour guide, announcer, referee, negotiator, psychologist, psychic, fortune teller, peacemaker, doctor, nurse, mechanic, organizer, expert on local and world affairs, politician, expert on personal development, guide to the underprivileged, teacher, parent, and shoulder to cry on.

"Working a steady run you get to know some of your passengers—which makes your day much easier because it allows for informal interaction with all kinds of people. I also like being outside, seeing the world go by, and not being touched by the elements. Another plus is that you never have to take your job home. The minute you walk away from the bus, your work is done."

Expert Advice

"People who are drawn to bus driving usually possess a certain quality that makes them want to deal with people from all walks of life. This is by far the most important prerequisite to becoming a happy bus driver. Once in a while you come across a grumpy old man, who has no interpersonal skills or compassion. This person was never meant to drive a bus; he should have hauled garbage instead.

"Another must is that you should enjoy driving. If bad drivers get under your skin, if you are impatient or lack compassion toward other people, you had better look for something more suitable. If you want to be a happy bus driver, you must possess the aforementioned qualities. Or you will become that old grouch."

INTERVIEW
Bobbie Ann Zielinski
School Bus Driver

Bobbie Ann Zielinski is a school bus driver for the school district's transportation department in Elgin, Illinois. She has been working as a driver since 1986.

How Bobbie Ann Zielinski Got Started

"My mother is in charge of a bus company and I started with her privately owned company at the age of nineteen as a bus driver's assistant. We worked with behaviorally disordered children and had to have an assistant on every bus to help the driver with the children so the driver could drive safely.

"I applied for my current job because I had gone to school in this district my whole life and wanted to give back a little that they gave me. I filled out an application. They looked at my qualifications, took me on a test drive, and I was hired.

"All bus companies have a driver/trainer at their facility to show you the ropes and teach the safety rules expected of you as a school bus driver. They teach you how to inspect your vehicle every day before you leave the lot to pick up the children. Then you go to the DMV and get tested there for your commercial driver's license. You take a number of written tests, a vehicle inspection test, a road test, and a backing test. It's quite difficult."

What the Job's Really Like

"Bus drivers get up very early to start their day. I rise at 4:30 A.M. and get to work by 5:45 A.M. I am in my bus by 6:15 and picking up my first group of kids by 6:45. After I deliver them safely to their school, I have four more schools to do the same with. I finish around 9:15 A.M. and unless I do a midday (preschoolers and kindergarten routes that go half days), I'm off until 1:00 P.M. Then I go back to work, bring home the kids I brought in, and finish by 4:30 P.M. I work approximately 7½ hours a day.

"I have two children and being a bus driver is the best for a working mom. You are off work the same days your children are off school. The sad part is that you never get to bring them to school on their first day or see them come home with excitement from a great day at school. It's also hard to go on class trips with them. I try my best though.

"While on the bus, you have many responsibilities and at times it can be very stressful. Sometimes you get hard-to-control kids, and you have to work with the school authorities and parents. We transport bilingual students and they can't understand everything you tell them, so you need someone to translate for you. You have to watch all other drivers on the road and keep in mind at all times that you are the professional out there and have to keep a cool head. You are a baby-sitter, a social worker, a friend, a teacher, and sometimes a parent to these children. And even though you have bad days, when that one student thanks you for being you and a parent thanks you for driving their child safely, it's all worthwhile!

"I love being with the children, especially the ones that need you the most. You begin to feel something warm for every one of them and they are never forgotten your whole life. They make little pictures for you and write notes to you and make you feel like you're making a difference in their lives.

"On the downside, you have people driving around you, going past your stop arm, not thinking about the child that could be running out in front of them. Everybody wants to beat the bus. You have snowy days and bad weather to contend with, and some days you just wish you would have stayed home.

"I get paid hourly and we swipe a clock. I get $15.02 an hour at my company. We are among the highest-paid drivers in Illinois. We are union. When you start at our company you get a lower salary and work your way up. At privately owned and nonunion companies, top pay is usually around $10 to $11 an hour for driving the big buses and $8 to $9 an hour driving the small buses."

Expert Advice

"First off, you can't be in it for the money. You have to really be thinking of the kids and your role of being there to guide them and keep them safe. You have to know that they come first at all times just as your own children would. Safety should always be first in a bus driver's mind."

INTERVIEW
Sheryl Kersmarki
School Bus Driver

Sheryl Kersmarki is a single run school bus driver for the Gloucester County public school system in Gloucester, Virginia. She has been driving children to and from school since 1993.

How Sheryl Kersmarki Got Started

"I have always enjoyed being around children. They need positive role models. I didn't have the greatest childhood but I did have a few adults who I seriously looked up to. They gave me advice, helping me through difficult times. I thought, here is my chance to give back.

"I got involved with this work because our daughter was having problems on the school bus for this area. The driver had not stopped a parent from boarding the bus and orally attacking her. My daughter was only in the first grade. Our children weren't getting along. I telephoned transportation to complain about this driver. While speaking to the head of this department, he baited me, 'If you think you can do a better job, come in and fill out an application. We can always use good drivers.' I jumped at the challenge. Children need to know someone out there cares, and all students have the right to feel safe on a bus.

"The county provides on-the-road training and in-class sessions that enable us to get our commercial driver's license, if we pass the class. My trainer was a wonderful lady named Beverly. I was and still am impressed with her knowledge of safety and her ability to care for students."

What the Job Is Really Like

"My job is simple. I take students back and forth to school each day safely. Safety comes first with me. You will never see my kids walking or moving around while that bus is rolling.

"I also expect that the children will get along with one another. It's a must in my eyes. If a kid has a problem with another child, we work it out with words, not fists. Sound too good to be true? Come see us sometime. Just look for the yellow bus that is full of smiling faces and laughter resounding out the windows.

"I didn't begin driving a bus for money. It's not something that will make you rich. I earn $6,100 per year as a single route driver. The wealth you take away each day is a smile of a child and a thank-you. I'd drive for just the hugs any day. I drove a little boy a couple of years back who lived with only his father. The women in his life were few and included only his baby-sitter, his elementary school teacher, and me. He hugged me twice a day, saying, 'I love you, Ms. K.' Now that is a reward.

"To this day, I still have every card, every picture drawn, and every gift given to me. (I kept a cherry lollipop for three years but the sugar broke down and attracted ants. I finally had to throw it away.)

"Driving is rewarding. You can make lasting impressions on a child's life. I am big on the importance of education. My kids actually do homework going down the road. By the time they get home, usually it is done. Now they have time to do whatever it is they do after school. They even had paired up to help each other. Sadly, I have driven kids who have dropped out of school. Each one has stayed in touch with me and all have received or are working on their GEDs. They said it was because of me. I don't know if this is the truth, but it sure is nice to think so.

"My life has been enriched because of them—all 414 of them. Yes, I can tell you each of their names, but I can't remember the day of the week.

"I spend a total of three hours a day on my bus. The rest of the day is mine to write, clean the house, or ride my horse. It is my choice. We have off whenever school is closed, including the summer, and get paid for it. Where else can a person do this? I am home when my daughter arrives home.

"The work is never boring. We try to have some fun on my bus. At one time I had an intercom system. We went down the back country roads blasting music from the outside speaker. During hunting season we'd yell out to deer, 'Run Bambi run, hunters are coming.' Or the kids would bark at dogs to get them out of the road—it was hilarious. Those poor dogs to this day don't chase yellow school buses. We did use the intercom for good things as well. At Christmas time, a different child was chosen every day to read a story to all the other children. This only worked with elementary students. The parties we have had were great. I try to have two parties a year. One for Christmas and an end-of-the-year blowout. We have sodas, cupcakes, cookies, chips, popcorn, pizza—whatever the kids decide. I used to make small Christmas stockings with each child's name. I would stuff them with goodies and hang them on the back of the seat in front of them.

"There are so many things I like about my job. The freedom it offers is a plus. The relationships built on trust have to be at the top of the list. The children I am lucky to drive have become like my own. I have been big sister, teacher, nurse, doctor, and friend all in one afternoon. I go above and beyond the duties required. I get up early on a snowy morning just to telephone all the students on my roster to let them know if school will be open or not. Most of my kids have parents who work and leave the house before their children do. When someone is out sick or hurt I make sure to phone them with a quick get well call. It only takes a moment of my time to do this but leaves that person feeling cared for.

"There are three downsides to this job. One is that there are never enough sub-drivers. Contract drivers have to drive ill or injured. If you need a sub, you'd better phone in quickly. The garage opens around 6:00 A.M., and within five minutes all subs are used. You are out of luck. But if you are lucky enough to get a sub, turn off your telephone. Transportation will hound you to come back in to work.

"Driving in inclement weather is also a downside. Wet or icy roads can be dangerous. One minute all is moving smoothly, the next your bus is sliding into a ditch. Thank the man above we don't get much snow here. I'd be in a ditch all the time.

"The third downside is getting emotionally attached to the kids. I drove this fabulous girl whose life was cut short in a car accident. She was only thirteen years old. I will always cherish the time she and I shared. She, along with a few other neighborhood kids, gave me a springer spaniel puppy after I had a miscarriage while driving my bus. I'll never forget her words: 'Now maybe you will smile again. We have missed you.' Smile? Oh, I did and then some. That puppy grew into the sweetest dog and still brings joy to my heart every day.

"Do I ever get in trouble with supervisors? All the time, but seeing a child's smile and sharing makes it all worthwhile. As long as my kids are safe and feel safe with me, I'll keep doing what I do."

Expert Advice

"A person must care for and enjoy being around children of all ages. Your heart must have room for each of your precious cargo. My kids come to me with their problems. I listen to each and advise them where they can seek the proper help. (We aren't allowed to give direct advice, but *you* try closing your heart to an innocent face.)

"Children need praise and need to hear, 'Hey, I'm proud of you!' On my run, I award my students for good grades. All A's earn a can of soda. Even an F gets a piece of gum if that child tried their best. So you see, you have to care.

"But you can't wear your heart on your sleeve. Kids can be cruel. Show them respect and they will return it to you tenfold.

"It is easy to get started in this line of work. You simply have to telephone the county or city's school board office and inquire about the transportation department. And don't let the size of that bus intimidate you. It is easy to maneuver. The county will not send drivers out on the road until they are at ease behind the wheel. Always put safety first. You have the lives of precious cargo—someone's child—in your hands.

"In Gloucester, Virginia, where I work, if you use drugs or alcohol, forget it. You will be wasting your time and theirs. They do random drug and alcohol testing and you are screened before any hiring takes place. How would you like your child being driven to school by a drug user?"

FOR MORE INFORMATION

For further information on employment opportunities, contact local transit systems, intercity bus lines, school systems, or the local offices of the state employment service.

General information on bus driving is available from:

American Bus Association
1100 New York Avenue NW, Suite 1050
Washington, DC 20005

General information on school bus driving is available from:

National School Transportation Association
P.O. Box 2639
Springfield, VA 22152

General information on local transit bus driving is available from:

American Public Transit Association
1201 New York Avenue NW, Suite 400
Washington, DC 20005

General information on motorcoach driving is available from:

United Motorcoach Association
113 S. West Street, 4th Floor
Alexandria, VA 22314

CHAPTER 2

Taxi Drivers and Chauffeurs

EDUCATION
H.S. preferred

$$$ SALARY/EARNINGS
$10,000 to $44,000

OVERVIEW

Anyone who has been in a large city knows the importance of taxicab and limousine service. Drivers pick up passengers from street corners, airports, bus terminals, and train stations and drive them to their destinations. Their service helps residents, commuters, and visitors get from one place to another in a timely fashion.

Taxi drivers, also known as cab drivers, drive taxicabs, which most frequently are large, conventional automobiles modified for commercial passenger transport. Drivers collect fares from passengers at standardized rates based on zone areas, miles traveled, or time spent to reach the destination. They record the length of each trip and the point of origin and destination on a log, or trip sheet. These logs help check the drivers' activity and efficiency.

At the start of their driving shift, cab drivers usually report to a cab service or garage where they are assigned a cab. They are given a trip sheet to record their name, work date, and cab identification number. Drivers check the cab's fuel and oil levels, and make sure the lights, brakes, and windshield wipers are in good working order. Drivers adjust rear and side mirrors and their seat for comfort. Any equipment or part not in good working order is reported to the dispatcher or company mechanic.

Taxi drivers pick up their passengers in one of three ways. Customers requesting transportation may call the cab company and give a location, an approximate pick-up time, and their destination. The cab company dispatcher then relays the information to a driver by two-way radio, cellular telephone, or on-board computer. In urban areas, drivers may cruise streets and pick up passengers who hail or "wave" them down. Drivers also may get passengers by waiting at cab stands or in taxi lines at airports, train stations, hotels, and other places where people frequently seek taxis.

Drivers should be familiar with streets in the areas they serve so they can use the most efficient route to destinations. They should also know the locations of frequently requested destinations, such as airports, bus and railroad terminals, convention centers, hotels, and other points of interest. In case of emergency, the driver should know the location of fire stations, police stations, and hospitals.

Upon reaching the destination, drivers determine the fare and announce it to the rider. Fares often consist of many parts. In many taxicabs, a taximeter measures the fare based on the length of the trip and the amount of time the trip took. Drivers turn the taximeter on when passengers enter the cab and turn it off when the they reach the final destination. The fare may also include a surcharge for additional passengers or for handling luggage, or an additional "drop charge" or flat fee added for the use of the cab. Along with paying the fare, most passengers will give the driver a tip. The amount of the gratuity depends on the passengers' satisfaction with the quality and efficiency of the ride and courtesy of the driver. A driver will issue a receipt upon request from the passenger. Drivers enter onto the trip sheet all information regarding the trip, including the place and time of pick-up and drop-off and the total fee. They also must fill out accident reports when necessary.

Chauffeurs operate limousines, vans, and private cars for limousine companies, private businesses, government agencies, and wealthy individuals. Many chauffeurs transport customers in large vans between hotels and airports, bus, or train terminals. Others drive luxury automobiles, such as limousines, to popular entertainment and social events. Still others provide full-time personal transportation for wealthy families and private companies.

At the start of the work day, chauffeurs ready their automobiles or vans for use. They inspect the vehicle for cleanliness and, when needed, vacuum the interior and wash the exterior body, windows, and mirrors. They check fuel and oil levels and make sure the lights, tires, brakes, and windshield wipers work. Chauffeurs may perform routine maintenance and make minor repairs, such as changing tires or adding oil and other fluids when needed. The chauffeur will take the vehicle to a professional mechanic if the vehicle requires more complicated repairs.

Chauffeurs cater to their passengers with attentive customer service and a special regard for detail. They help riders into the car by holding open doors, holding umbrellas when raining, and loading packages and luggage into the trunk of the car. They may perform errands for their employers such as delivering packages or picking up items. Drivers are also hired to meet clients who arrive at airports. Many chauffeurs offer conveniences and luxuries in their limousines to ensure a pleasurable ride, such as newspapers, music, drinks, televisions, and telephones.

Taxi drivers and chauffeurs occasionally have to load and unload heavy luggage and packages. Driving for long periods of time can be tiring, especially in densely populated urban areas, and driving in bad weather, heavy traffic, or mountainous and hilly areas can be nerve-racking. Sitting for long periods of time can be uncomfortable. Drivers must be alert to conditions on the road, especially in heavy and congested traffic or in bad weather. They must also take precautions to prevent accidents and avoid sudden stops, turns, and other driving maneuvers that would jar the passenger.

Work hours of taxi drivers and chauffeurs vary greatly. Some jobs offer full-time or part-time employment with work hours that can change from day to day or remain the same every day. It is often necessary for drivers to report to work on short notice. Chauffeurs who work for a single employer may be on call much of the time. Evening and weekend work are common for limousine and taxicab services.

The needs of the client or employer dictate the work schedule for chauffeurs. The work of taxi drivers is much less structured. Working free from supervision, they may break for a meal or a rest whenever their vehicle is unoccupied. However, taxi drivers risk robbery because they work alone and often carry large amounts of cash.

Full-time taxi drivers usually work one shift a day, which may last from eight to twelve hours. Part-time drivers may work half a shift each day, or work a full shift once or twice a week. Drivers must be on duty at all times of the day and night, because most taxi companies offer services twenty-four hours a day. Early morning and late night shifts are common. Drivers work long hours during holidays, weekends, and other special events to support heavier demand for their services. Independent drivers, however, often set their own hours and schedules.

Design improvements in newer cabs have reduced stress and increased the efficiency of drivers. Many are equipped with tracking devices, fare meters, and dispatching equipment. Satellites and tracking systems link many of these state-of-the-art vehicles with company headquarters. Directions, traffic advisories, weather reports, and other important communications can be delivered to the driver anywhere in the transporting area in a matter of seconds. The satellite link-up also allows the dispatcher to track the vehicle's location, fuel consumption, and engine performance. Drivers can easily communicate with the dispatcher to discuss delivery schedules and courses of action should there be mechanical problems. When threatened with crime or violence, drivers may be able to alert authorities of emergency situations and have help arrive quickly.

Taxi drivers and chauffeurs meet many different types of people. Dealing with rude customers and waiting for passengers requires patience. Many municipalities and taxicab and chauffeur companies require dress codes. Typically, cities require taxicab drivers to wear clean and neat clothes. Many chauffeurs wear more formal attire, such as a tuxedo, a coat and tie, a dress, or a uniform and cap.

TRAINING

Local governments set license standards and requirements for taxi drivers and chauffeurs. Although requirements vary, most municipalities have minimum qualifications for driving experience and training. Many taxi and limousine companies set higher standards than the ones required by law. It is common for an applicant's medical, credit, criminal, and driving record to be reviewed. In addition, many companies require a higher minimum age and prefer that drivers be high school graduates.

People interested in driving a limousine or taxicab must first have a regular automobile driver's license. They also must acquire a chauffeur or taxi driver's license, commonly called a "hack" license. Local authorities generally require applicants for a hack license to pass a written exam or complete a training program. To qualify either through an exam or a training program, applicants must know local geography, motor vehicle laws, safe driving practices, regulations governing taxicabs, and display some aptitude for being able to deal courteously with the public. Training programs usually include a test on English proficiency, usually in the form of listening comprehension; applicants who do not pass the English exam must take an English course along with the formal driving program. Many taxicab or limousine companies sponsor applicants and give them a temporary permit that allows them to drive, even though they may not yet have finished the training program or passed the test.

Some taxi and limousine companies give new drivers on-the-job training. They show drivers how to operate the taximeter and communications equipment, and how to complete paperwork. Other topics covered may include driver safety and popular sightseeing and entertainment destinations. Many companies have contracts with social service agencies and transportation services to transport elderly and disabled citizens in nonemergency situations. To support these services, new drivers may get special training on how to handle wheelchair lifts and other mechanical devices.

Taxi drivers and chauffeurs should be able to get along with many different types of people. They must be patient when waiting for passengers or when dealing with rude customers, and driving in heavy and congested traffic requires tolerance and a mild temperament. Drivers should also be dependable because passengers rely on them to be picked up at prearranged times and taken to the correct destination. To be successful, drivers must be responsible and self-motivated because they work with little supervision.

The majority of taxi drivers and chauffeurs are called "lease drivers." Lease drivers pay a monthly or weekly fee to the company allowing them to lease their vehicle and have access to the company dispatch system. The fee may also include a charge for vehicle maintenance, insurance, and a deposit on the vehicle. Lease drivers may take their cars home with them when they are not on duty.

Opportunities for advancement are limited for taxi drivers and chauffeurs. Experienced drivers may obtain preferred routes or shifts. Some advance to dispatcher or manager jobs; others may start their own limousine company. On the other hand, many drivers like the independent, unsupervised work of driving their automobile.

In many small- and medium-size communities, drivers are able to buy their taxi, limousine, or other type of automobile and go into business for themselves. These independent owner-drivers require an additional permit that allows them to operate their vehicle as a company. Some big cities limit the number of operating permits and one may only become an owner-driver by buying a permit from an owner-driver who is leaving the business. Although many owner-drivers are successful, some fail to cover expenses and eventually lose their permit and automobile. Good business sense and courses in accounting, business, and business arithmetic can help an owner-driver become successful. Knowledge of mechanics can enable owner-drivers to perform their routine maintenance and minor repairs to cut expenses.

JOB OUTLOOK

Taxi drivers and chauffeurs held about 106,000 jobs in 1996. About two-thirds were wage and salary workers employed by a company or business. Of these, about 33 percent worked for local and suburban transportation companies and about 20 percent worked for taxicab companies. Others worked for automotive rental dealerships, private households, and funeral homes. About a third were self-employed.

People seeking jobs as taxi drivers and chauffeurs should encounter good opportunities. Thousands of job openings will occur each year as drivers transfer to other occupations or leave the labor force. However, driving jobs vary greatly in terms of earnings, work hours, and working conditions. Because driving does not require education beyond high school, competition is expected for jobs offering regular hours and attractive earnings and working conditions. Opportunities should be best for persons with good driving records who are able to work flexible schedules.

Employment of taxi drivers and chauffeurs is expected to grow slower than the average for all occupations through 2006 as local and intercity travel increases with population growth. Opportunities should be best in metropolitan areas that are growing rapidly.

Job opportunities can fluctuate from season to season and from month to month. Extra drivers may be hired during holiday seasons and peak travel and tourist times. During economic slowdowns, drivers are seldom laid off but they may have to increase their working hours, and earnings may decline somewhat. Independent owner-operators are particularly vulnerable to economic slowdowns.

SALARIES

Earnings of taxi drivers and chauffeurs vary greatly, depending on the number of hours worked, customers' tips, and other factors. Those who usually worked full-time had median weekly earnings of $387 in 1996. The middle 50 percent earned between $258 and $653 a week. The lowest 10 percent earned less than $192, while the highest 10 percent earned more than $850 a week. Earnings were generally higher in more urban areas.

According to limited information available, the majority of independent taxi owner-drivers earned from about $20,000 to $30,000, including tips. However, professional drivers with a regular clientele often earn more. Many chauffeurs who worked full-time earned from about $25,000 to $50,000, including tips.

RELATED FIELDS

Other workers who drive vehicles on highways and city streets are ambulance drivers, bus drivers, and truck drivers.

INTERVIEW
Sarah Benson
Taxi Driver

Sarah Benson is an owner-operator of a taxi that she drives through the Grand Old Taxi company in Nashville, Tennessee. She has been a driver since 1989.

How Sarah Benson Got Started

"I had been working for an insurance company but had been under a great deal of stress, so I decided to try something entirely different. Because I was a single parent at the time, it was important that I find another job immediately. I checked into driving a taxi and learned that with little expense and almost no training I could be working before my severance pay ran out.

"In some cities there is an extensive training period for new taxi drivers. But here in Nashville they expect you to have lived in the area for about three years so you know your way around. You are required to take a 2½ hour training session provided by the metropolitan agency that is responsible for the taxi industry. And you are expected to ride with another driver for at least a few hours to learn to use the radio, locate taxi stands, and do the limited amount of paperwork that is required of taxi drivers. After one day I was on my own. Basically, if you didn't have a wreck the first day you were considered a "good" driver.

"My husband and I now own a taxi that we operate about sixteen to twenty hours per day. I drive in the daytime and my husband drives in the evenings."

What the Job's Really Like

"As an owner-operator my expenses include the cost of the car and maintenance as well as fuel and insurance. I also pay the taxi company through which I work a weekly fee for advertising, radio service, etc. The total weekly cost to operate my taxi is about $400 per week, but this doesn't include fuel. My fuel usually costs from $5 to $15 per day depending on how busy I am, but it never exceeds 5 or 6 percent of my gross income.

"My primary duty is picking up people at the airport, hotels, restaurants, homes, businesses, bus stations—anywhere they are—and taking them where they need or want to go.

"On a typical day I get up around 4:00 A.M., have a bowl of cereal and a cup of coffee, and check in with the dispatcher. Since not all taxi drivers get up early, this is often a very profitable time. Our company has an account with a state healthcare provider, so I usually pick up a lady to go to dialysis at 5:30 A.M.

"Our dispatcher is able to obtain information regarding checkouts at the major hotels so I often find someone going to the airport. After I drop the person at the airport, I may stay at the airport to wait for another fare. (It isn't a good idea to drive a long distance between every fare because you can use up too much fuel.) With experience you learn to know where you can expect people to need your services, but sometimes, I would have to say, you also get a 'feeling' about business and it's usually a good idea to go with those feelings. For instance, I may take someone from the airport to Brentwood, Tennessee, which is just south of Nashville. We don't get a lot of calls from that area, but I have driven by one of the hotels there and found someone looking for transportation to the airport or into Nashville.

"The taxi business can be busy and interesting, but it can also be slow and boring. I enjoy people so it is usually interesting to me. I have met people from all over the world who come here either for business or because of the country music industry.

"One of our busiest times is during Fan Fare each year in June, when the country stars are all performing here and signing autographs for fans. This is also a very profitable time for me because people who have been saving for years to come to Fan Fare will pay whatever they have to pay to get to where their favorite star is performing.

"Another reason the taxi business is interesting is that sometimes we have an opportunity to meet and provide transportation for celebrities. Some of the ones I have met are Jon Voight, Foster Brooks, Tommy Lasorda, and numerous producers and agents whose names are not household words. I once saw President Jimmy Carter and his wife get into a taxi in front of me at the airport.

"Some of my passengers have been mayors, governors, policemen, and other public figures from Nashville, as well as other cities and states.

"In addition to the 'strangers' I meet every day, there are several local people who travel in business who are my regular customers. For their convenience, and mine, I have a cellular phone so they can contact me at any time. Sometimes I receive a call from 'Mr. Smith in Denver' giving me the date, time, and flight number for his arrival so I can pick him up at the airport.

"One of the downsides is that the taxi business is a dangerous business. We have about one taxi driver per year robbed or murdered here in Nashville, so obviously safety is one of our primary concerns. There are several things you can do to lessen the possibility of having a terrible experience. First, you have to constantly be aware of where you are and what is happening around you. You might be dispatched to a residence to pick up a fare; if you arrive to find a person standing on the street or if someone comes from around the side of the house after you arrive you should drive past them until you are out of sight. If the call is legitimate, they will call the dispatcher and wait until you get back around the block. If it is just someone using the address to get a taxi driver (whom they expect to be carrying cash), you have just avoided a potentially dangerous situation.

"Speaking of money: The taxi business can be very profitable when business is good so it is important to stop at your bank and make frequent deposits or drop by the house to leave money in a safe place. If you pick up someone who has the intention of robbing you, it is probably best to have little money with you and to give over what you have.

"Some taxi drivers have permits to carry guns, but this is controversial. While it may provide a degree of protection, there is always the possibility that a gun may be taken from you by a robber and used against you. Personally, I do not carry a gun but I have something in my car that could be used as a weapon if needed.

"A lot of people have the mistaken impression that all taxi drivers are greedy. Some are, and I suppose I am at times, but I also provide free transportation for people from time to time. For instance, I'll be on my way to a hotel when I see someone walking in the rain. I usually stop and ask them if they would like a free ride. (I'm going there anyway so it doesn't cost me anything, and frequently that person will call me when they need to go somewhere later.)

"I spend an average of eight to ten hours a day operating the taxi, but I have worked as much as sixteen hours, the maximum allowed without a break. However, one of the nice things about this industry, especially for owner-operators, is that I can take a day off when I want.

"I like the flexibility of working the hours I prefer to work, and about the only thing I don't like is that sometimes business is slow. Plus, there's always the odd person who treats you badly or the one who 'trashes' your taxi. There are people who will put cigarette butts out on the upholstery if you allow them to smoke in your taxi. Others will drop all kinds of trash on the floor. (Sometimes they also drop money, but I don't mind cleaning that up.) Most of the customers are nice, but there are some who aren't, especially those who have the opinion that taxi drivers are so stupid they are unable to find other work to do."

Expert Advice

"Anyone who wishes to be successful in the taxi business must like dealing with people and have a pleasant manner; otherwise the tips will be few. Not getting a tip is terrible for morale!

"You also must like driving in traffic, or at least be able to deal with driving in traffic without losing your cool.

"It is also necessary to have a good sense of direction and be good at finding your way around. You have to be able to locate alternate routes when you encounter gridlock situations.

"You also need to know which restaurants are good and which to avoid; which stars are performing during any given week; what sports events are taking place; the days and hours of operation for museums; what cultural events are taking place, and just about any other information that is available about the area you're in.

"I would not advise anyone to get into this business unless he or she has the self-discipline required to be independent. You also have to be able to deal with making a lot of money one day and none the next, because that is sometimes the way the business is."

INTERVIEW
Timothy Sexton
Taxi Driver

Timothy Sexton is a taxicab driver in Reno, Nevada. He has worked in this field for more than fifteen years. He is also a certified auto mechanic.

How Timothy Sexton Got Started

"I was in the U.S. Navy in the 1970s and I rode cabs regularly in San Diego, California. I was always amazed at how the cab drivers knew the town and got me where I was going safely.

"In Reno I just applied for the job, and after talking to the general manager, was accepted on the spot.

"My training was strictly on-the-job. I had to learn how to follow directions from the dispatcher as well as how to read a map book."

What the Job's Really Like

"My duties as a taxicab driver are working with the public during my twelve-hour shift. I must put up with all kinds of people—meaning ones who have had too much to drink, or are in various moods. You also have many nice people, too.

"Driving a taxi is a tedious job. You take verbal abuse from your customers because the customer is always right. You have to be on your toes at all times because the customers are always trying to run scams on you. You have customers who really do not want to pay for their ride. You are always accused of going the long way.

"The first order of business in my workday is to take my codriver home and then I head downtown to one of the local casino cab stands and wait for a customer. We also have computer dispatch, and you have the option of using the computer or not. At this point in time I rarely take dispatch calls. I do have a cellular phone so regular customers can contact me. I spend my day waiting at the cab stand for customers. I basically let the customer come to me and take them from point A to point B.

"The day can be interesting when you have a lot of trips and you are making a lot of money. It's also interesting when you are meeting people from a variety of different countries and all walks of life—it makes for interesting conversation. But you have many days when you may sit for an hour waiting for a fare and then they only want to go three or four blocks.

"I work anywhere from seventy to eighty-four hours per week. Sometimes I may take a half of a day off if business is really slow.

"My job consists of getting out and opening doors for the elderly and female passengers. I also load luggage in the trunk of my vehicle. I am supposed to be a walking road map. I should know every street in the city. I should always be courteous to my customers. I should dress neatly and bathe regularly. I should have a clean car. I should obey the driving laws set forth by the city, county, state, and federal government.

"I like the freedom of my job—being allowed to make as much money as I want to. The company I work for made us independent contractors about six years ago. I make somewhere between $30,000 to $32,000 yearly, but I have to pay for my own gasoline and pay a weekly lease to the cab company. My lease at this time is $482 per week, and my codriver, the person I share the cab with, pays half of that. It costs me about $65 per week for fuel. After figuring my lease payment and gasoline my net pay is $12,000 to $14,000. Taking care of your own taxes and Social Security can be a nightmare.

"What I like the least about my work is knowing that I could be killed at any time for a very small amount of money. The taxi industry is rated as being the most dangerous job. You must be prepared at all times for anything and everything. Luckily, I have never been robbed, but I have been put in some very scary situations over the years.

"When I was driving for Red Top Taxi in Modesto, California, I was dispatched to an apartment complex to pick up a customer. We proceeded on about a three-block ride. She told me to pull over to a bar, so I did. As I came to a stop, the police turned on their microphone and told everyone in the taxi to keep our hands where they could be seen. The officers came over to the taxi with their guns drawn. They told my customer to step out of the taxi with her hands above her head. They then promptly arrested her. But at least they had her pay the cab fare. Later on, I found out she had stabbed her boyfriend or husband with a butcher knife.

"Another time, in Reno, I picked up two passengers at one of the downtown casinos. They wanted to go to the mall. On the way, I noticed we were being followed by an old Ford pickup. I changed lanes to see if my suspicions were correct. The pickup changed lanes and continued following me. At our destination, the pickup pulled in front of me, blocking me. I had no idea what was going on. All of a sudden the doors of the pickup opened and several people came running over to my cab. Turns out my passengers were rock stars and the people following us were fans. We all got autographs. But only my daughter knew who they were. I'm not into rock music.

"That started out scary, but ended up comical. Another time it wasn't so funny. I got a good fare to go quite a distance, with a few stops on the way. He told me he was going to San Francisco to his sister's and then was going on a blind date. He had given me $100 up front and told me that that was mine for sure. He changed his destination from Stockton Airport to the mall so he could buy some presents for his sister's children. At the mall he handed me another $60 and told me to take my wife to dinner that evening.

"On the way home, I was told by dispatch that my presence was requested where I had picked up my last customer. I got there and found city and county cops and FBI agents swarming the place. They asked numerous questions about my fare, his description, his clothing, and where our final destination had been. They confiscated the money the fare had paid me and gave me a receipt.

"The next day I read about the bank robber who was 'armed and dangerous' and had escaped in a taxicab. I later was contacted again by the FBI and was shown some mug shots. I identified the person. I asked about my money and was told that if and when he was caught, after he got out of prison, he would have to make restitution of the $160. They didn't have to give it to me, it was the bank's money.

"Not taking this lying down and this being close to Christmas, I contacted various state and federal agencies but was told 'tough luck.' I then wrote a letter to the editor of the newspaper. I titled it 'Who Does the Money Belong To?'

"As it turned out, because the bills were $20s, the money belonged to me. After the article came out on a Saturday I was called on Monday to come and pick up my money. As far as I know, the bank robber was never caught and the money he stole never recovered."

Expert Advice

"Someone just starting in this business should be prepared to work for less than the minimum wage. You should be prepared to be abused verbally. You should be prepared to be a caring driver and be very 'customer conscious.'

"You should be able to speak English well and be able to read a map book. You should be able to follow directions and conduct yourself in a pleasant manner.

"The best advice I can give for this occupation is think long and hard about being in a job where you might have to put your life on the line. And if you are ever put in a robbery situation, give your money up right away and pray that they spare your life."

INTERVIEW
Lawrence Shepard
Chauffeur

Lawrence Shepard has been a chauffeur for McPherson Enterprises, Limited in Towson, Maryland, since 1996. He has an A.A. in general studies from Central Texas College in Killeen, Texas, and military police training from his previous career in the U.S. Army.

How Lawrence Shepard Got Started

"I was attracted to this position by the pay, $35,000 a year, and I like to drive and see various places. I had taken defensive driving courses in the military for police work so I was qualified.

"I found my job through a help wanted ad I saw in the *Baltimore Sun*. My boss asked me if I had any administrative knowledge when I interviewed. My job involves more than just being a chauffeur. I had plenty of experience, from being a platoon sergeant in the army and from writing police-type reports in the military. I also was a recruiter for a while and ran an office in Baltimore, giving me complete knowledge of the Baltimore and D.C. areas. My last job at the Pentagon for the army was on General Colin Powell's personal security team. I knew how to run all types of different computer systems and software, a good fit for my current boss's needs. You have to be versatile or present yourself as versatile to fit."

What the Job's Really Like

"I am responsible for driving up to three cars, and seeing that the general maintenance gets completed. I do a lot of driving between Baltimore, Richmond, Virginia, the Washington, D.C. area, and Northern Virginia.

"A typical day is to be on the road by 4:45 A.M. on my way to my boss's house. From his house, we either travel back to the office or head to our first appointment.

"We have a full office set up in the car so, while he is on appointments, I am on the computer retrieving items needed for the next appointment or working on correspondence for various appointments. So, in addition to driving, I also get to do on-the-spot administrative-type work. We have a laptop, printer, and fax, so I can accomplish these tasks.

"I also am responsible for reading several publications to glean information regarding potential clients. In addition, I research various companies to determine the true owner and the value of the company and its annual income.

"My boss is a financial/estate planner. He also sells insurance and does very detailed tax planning. He does this work primarily for people who have significant wealth. Before he hired me, he spent too much time driving between appointments and not getting anything else done. Now he can work in the back of the car while I drive.

"My boss's appointments generally last about an hour and a half or so and finish up for the day around 3:00 or 3:30 P.M., at which time I transport him home. I then get home between 6:30 and 7:00 P.M.

"My boss travels out of the area a lot, so some days when he's gone, I help around the office doing whatever needs to be done. I also check his house while he is on vacation or at a convention.

"To me, the days are laid back and relaxed, especially compared to my military career. But some days the driving can be hectic. The roads, expressways, and beltways in the Baltimore–Washington–Northern Virginia area are bumper to bumper during rush hours. So we have to plan my boss's appointments wisely. This is why we start so early. Our first appointment is usually at 7:00 A.M.

"I never get bored because I always find something to do. The people I meet are very interesting and most are entrepreneurs—self-made millionaires.

"When my boss is out of town I generally get to the office by 8:00 A.M. and leave by 2:00 or 3:00 P.M. because there just isn't that much to do. But, when he is there I work about fifty to sixty hours per week. It all averages out to about forty hours per week.

"I like the driving the most as I get to see a lot of the nation's capital and meet interesting clients. Plus, I am by myself and only have to worry about what I'm doing right or wrong and not forty to fifty people, like I had to do in the military. I am only responsible for myself, my own work, and ensuring that my boss gets to his destinations safely.

"But I don't like coming home during rush hour because it takes way longer than it should. My boss used to live forty-five minutes from my home. Now he lives two hours away. I don't like getting home later than 5:00 P.M. because I umpire baseball and coach the local high school wrestling team in my spare time.

"I'm retired from the military and I'm just trying to have fun now. I don't want to do anything dangerous, like being a police officer in Baltimore. I really enjoy my work."

Expert Advice

"You'll need to know how to drive a big car and how to drive well and safely. If possible, you should take some driving courses. Any type of past taxi driving or delivery driving could be helpful. This would give you a general idea of the area and how to get around.

"You should be courteous, patient, prompt, and willing to provide service with a smile. Nothing is the boss's fault; it's always yours, even though you know it isn't."

INTERVIEW
Artemio Gonzalez, Jr.
Personal Chauffeur

Artemio Gonzalez, Jr., has been a chauffeur for CAI Advisors in New York City since 1992.

How Artemio Gonzalez, Jr., Got Started

"I was out of work for a year. A friend of mine knew one of the drivers for the company and said they were looking for someone. I drove for my employer for three months before I was hired permanently.

What the Job's Really Like

"The job is, at times, lonely. My duties are to pick up my employer at 7:30 A.M., or earlier if he's going to a meeting. I finish around 6:00 P.M. but sometimes, if he goes to dinner or the theater or opera, I finish about 10:00 or 12:00 P.M.

"I spend a typical day patiently waiting in my car. I don't even go up to the office to relax or use the bathroom.

"Sometimes I enjoy being alone, with no one bothering me. But I would like to be more active. I feel that my other talents are being wasted. The reason I stay is because the money is good and I do get a lot of free time. Also my boss is a nice guy and treats me well.

"The biggest problem I have with this job is the lack of a permanent schedule. You never know what hours you're going to be working. If you're in a relationship, it will suffer if you don't have an understanding wife or girlfriend. I have lost a few girlfriends because I could never give them the quality time they deserved.

"I am in the process of starting a mail-order business from the car. With all that free time, why not? With the help of a laptop, I am setting everything up. I hope my website will be up and running soon.

"I do get some perks, like going to big functions and seeing people socialize and having fun, or getting to drive right up on the runway at the airport.

"But I wish they would establish a place where all chauffeurs could use a clean bathroom, relax, and converse with one another. Also, the lack of exercise is a big problem. I have gained fifty pounds in the seven years that I have worked at this job.

"I normally work around fifty to seventy hours a week. During the holidays it may be more. There's a lot of stress on this job and high blood pressure because of it. You worry about getting tickets, getting stopped by cops, getting the car towed, always looking over your shoulder, wondering if you're going to get car-jacked or held up or tons of other things, such as avoiding accidents. I must avoid at least ten a day.

"I do want to move on but I won't make what I am making now in a new job. I earn more than $35,000 a year."

Expert Advice

"You must have patience and expect not to make a great deal of money right away. You must have good driving skills and be able to think ahead to avoid a potential problem on the road.

"To get started, it helps to know someone. Or you could get lucky and find the right job advertised in the newspaper. Usually, though, a person recommends another person for a personal chauffeur position.

"To work for a car service or hired chauffeurs by the hour, just go to the companies and apply."

FOR MORE INFORMATION

Information on licensing and registration of taxi drivers and chauffeurs is available from offices of local governments that regulate taxicabs.

For information about work opportunities as a taxi driver or chauffeur, contact local taxi or limousine services or state employment service offices. For general information about the work of taxi drivers, contact:

International Taxicab and Livery Association
3849 Farragut Avenue
Kensington, MD 20895

For general information about the work of limousine drivers, contact:

National Limousine Association
900 North Pitt Street, Suite 220
Alexandria, VA 22314

CHAPTER 3 Truck Drivers

EDUCATION
H.S. preferred

$$$ SALARY/EARNINGS
$17,000 to $30,000

OVERVIEW

Throughout the day and night, trucks transport everything from milk to automobiles. Due to a truck's ability to link with rail, sea, or air transportation facilities, truck drivers usually make the initial pickup from factories, consolidate cargo at terminals for intercity shipment, and deliver goods from terminals to stores and homes. Indeed, trucks move nearly all goods at some point in their journey from producers to consumers.

Before leaving the terminal or warehouse, truck drivers check their trucks for fuel and oil. They also inspect the trucks to make sure the brakes, windshield wipers, and lights are working and that a fire extinguisher, flares, and other safety equipment are aboard and in working order. Drivers adjust mirrors so that both sides of the truck are visible from the driver's seat, and make sure cargo will not shift during the trip. Drivers report to the dispatcher any equipment that does not work or is missing, or cargo that is not loaded properly.

Once underway, drivers must be alert to prevent accidents. Because drivers of large tractor-trailers sit higher than cars, pickups, and vans, they can see farther down the road. They seek traffic lanes that allow them to move at a steady speed, while keeping sight of varying road conditions.

The length of deliveries varies according to the merchandise being transported and the goods' final destination. Local drivers provide daily service for a specific route while other drivers provide intercity and interstate services that may vary from job to job. The drivers' responsibilities and assignments reflect the time spent on the road and the type of payloads they transport.

On short "turnarounds," truck drivers deliver a shipment to a nearby city, pick up another loaded trailer, and drive it back to their home base the same day; other runs take an entire day and keep drivers on the road overnight. On longer runs, drivers may haul loads from city to city for a week or more before returning home. Some companies use two drivers on very long runs. One drives while the other sleeps in a berth behind the cab. "Sleeper" runs may last for days, or even weeks, usually with the truck stopping only for fuel, food, and loading and unloading.

Some long-distance drivers who have regular runs transport freight to the same city on a regular basis. Many drivers perform unscheduled runs because shippers request varying service to different cities every day. Dispatchers tell these drivers when to report for work and where to haul the freight.

After long-distance truck drivers reach their destination or complete their operating shift, the U.S. Department of Transportation requires they complete reports detailing the trip, the condition of the truck, and the circumstances of any accidents. In addition, federal regulations require employers to subject drivers to random alcohol and drug tests while on duty.

Long-distance truck drivers spend most of their working time behind the wheel, but may load or unload their cargo after arriving at the final destination. This is especially common when drivers haul specialty cargo, because they may be the only one at the destination familiar with this procedure or certified to handle the materials. Auto-transport drivers, for example, drive and position cars on the trailers and head ramps and remove them at the dealerships. When picking up or delivering furniture, drivers of long-distance moving vans hire local workers to help them load or unload.

When local truck drivers receive assignments from the dispatcher to make deliveries, pickups, or both, they also get delivery forms. Before the drivers arrive for work, material handlers generally have loaded the trucks and arranged the items in order of delivery to minimize handling of the merchandise.

Local truck drivers usually load or unload the merchandise at the customer's place of business. Drivers may have helpers if there are many deliveries to make during the day or if the load requires heavy moving.

Customers must sign receipts for goods and pay the drivers the balance due on the merchandise if there is a cash-on-delivery arrangement. At the end of the day, drivers turn in receipts, money, records of deliveries made, and report any mechanical problems on their trucks.

The work of local truck drivers varies depending on the product they transport. Produce truckers usually pick up a loaded truck early in the morning and spend the rest of the day delivering produce to many different grocery stores. Lumber truck drivers, on the other hand, make several trips from the lumber yard to one or more construction sites. Gasoline tank truck drivers attach the hoses and operate the pumps on their trucks to transfer the gasoline to gas stations' storage tanks.

Some local truck drivers have sales and customer relations responsibilities. The primary responsibility of "driver–sales workers," or "route drivers," is to deliver their firm's products and represent the company in a positive manner. Their reaction to customer complaints and requests for special services makes the difference between a large order and a lost customer. Route drivers also use their selling ability to increase sales and gain additional customers.

The duties of driver–sales workers vary according to their industry, the policies of their particular company, and the emphasis placed on their sales responsibility. Most have wholesale routes that deliver to businesses and stores rather than homes. For example, wholesale bakery driver–sales workers deliver and arrange bread, cakes, rolls, and other baked goods on display racks in grocery stores. They estimate the amount and variety of baked goods to stock by paying close attention to the items that sell well, and those sitting on the shelves. They may recommend changes in a store's order or may encourage the manager to stock new bakery products.

Driver–sales workers employed by laundries that rent linens, towels, work clothes, and other items visit businesses regularly to replace soiled laundry. From time to time, they solicit new orders from businesses along their route.

Vending machine driver–sales workers service machines in factories, schools, and other buildings. They check items remaining in the machines, replace stock, and remove money deposited in the cash boxes. They also examine each vending machine to make minor repairs, clean machines, and to see that merchandise and change are dispensed properly.

After completing their route, driver–sales workers order items for the next delivery based on what products have been selling well, the weather, time of year, and any customer feedback.

Truck driving has become less physically demanding because most trucks now have more comfortable seats, better ventilation, and improved ergonomically designed cabs. However, driving for many hours at a stretch, unloading cargo, and making many deliveries can be tiring. Local truck drivers, unlike long-distance drivers, usually return home in the evening. Some self-employed long-distance truck drivers who own and operate their trucks spend over 240 days a year away from home.

Design improvements in newer trucks are reducing stress and increasing the efficiency of long-distance drivers. Many are a virtual mini-apartment on wheels, equipped with refrigerators, televisions, and bunks. Satellites and tracking systems link many of these state-of-the-art vehicles with company headquarters. Troubleshooting, directions, weather reports, and other important communications can be delivered to the truck anywhere in the country in a matter of seconds. Drivers can easily communicate with the dispatcher to discuss delivery schedules and courses of action, should there be mechanical problems. The satellite link-up also allows the dispatcher to track the truck's location, fuel consumption, and engine performance.

Local truck drivers frequently work forty-eight or more hours a week. Many who handle food for chain grocery stores, produce markets, or bakeries drive at night or early morning. Although most drivers have a regular route, some have different routes each day. Many local truck drivers, particularly driver–sales workers, load and unload their own trucks. This requires considerable lifting, carrying, and walking each day.

The U.S. Department of Transportation governs work hours and other matters of trucking companies engaged in interstate commerce. For example, a long-distance driver cannot work more than sixty hours in any seven-day period. Federal regulations also require that truckers rest eight hours for every ten hours of driving. Many drivers, particularly on long runs, work close to the maximum time permitted because they are typically compensated by the number of miles or hours they drive.

Drivers on long runs may face boredom, loneliness, and fatigue. Drivers frequently travel at night, on holidays, and weekends to avoid traffic delays and deliver cargo on time.

TRAINING

State and federal regulations govern the qualifications and standards for truck drivers. All drivers must comply with federal regulations and any state regulations exceeding federal requirements.

Truck drivers must have a driver's license issued by the state in which they live, and most employers require a clean driving record. Drivers of trucks designed to carry at least 26,000 pounds—including most tractor-trailers as well as bigger straight trucks—must obtain a commercial driver's license (CDL) from the state in which they live. All truck drivers who operate trucks transporting hazardous materials must obtain a CDL regardless of truck size. Federal regulations governing the CDL exempt certain groups including farmers, emergency medical technicians, firefighters, some military drivers, and snow and ice removers. In many states, a regular driver's license is sufficient for driving light trucks and vans.

To qualify for a commercial driver's license, applicants must pass a written test on rules and regulations, and then demonstrate they can operate a commercial truck safely. A national data bank permanently records all driving violations incurred by people who hold commercial licenses. A state will check these records and not issue a commercial driver's license to a driver who already has a license suspended or revoked in another state. Licensed drivers must accompany trainees until they get their own CDL. Information on how to apply for a commercial driver's license may be obtained from state motor vehicle administrations.

While many states allow those who are eighteen years and older to drive trucks within state borders, the U.S. Department of Transportation establishes minimum qualifications for truck drivers engaged in interstate commerce. Federal Motor Carrier Safety Regulations require that drivers must be at least twenty-one years old and pass a physical examination once every two years. The main physical requirements include good hearing, 20/40 vision with or without glasses or corrective lenses, and a seventy-degree field of vision in each eye. Drivers cannot be color blind. Drivers must be able to hear a forced whisper in one ear at not less than five feet, with or without a hearing aid. Drivers must have normal use of arms and legs and normal blood pressure. Drivers cannot use any controlled substances, unless prescribed by a licensed physician. People with epilepsy or diabetes controlled by insulin are not permitted to be interstate truck drivers. Federal regulations also require employers to test their drivers for alcohol and drug use as a condition of employment, and require periodic random tests while on duty. In addition, a driver must not have been convicted of a felony involving the use of a motor vehicle; a crime using drugs; driving under the influence of drugs or alcohol; or hit-and-run driving that resulted in injury or death.

All drivers must be able to read and speak English well enough to read road signs, prepare reports, and communicate with law enforcement officers and the public. Also, drivers must take a written examination on the Motor Carrier Safety Regulations of the U.S. Department of Transportation.

Many trucking operations have higher standards than those described. Many firms require that drivers be at least twenty-five years old, be able to lift heavy objects, and have driven trucks for three to five years. Many prefer to hire high school graduates and require annual physical examinations.

Because drivers often deal directly with the company's customers, they must get along well with people. For jobs as driver–sales workers, employers emphasize the ability to speak well, a neat appearance, self-confidence, initiative, and tact. Employers also look for responsible, self-motivated individuals able to work with little supervision.

Driver training courses are a desirable method of preparing for truck driving jobs and for obtaining a commercial driver's license. High school courses in driver training and automotive mechanics may also be helpful. Many private and public technical-vocational schools offer tractor-trailer driver training programs. Students learn to inspect the trucks and freight for compliance with federal, state, and local regulations. They also learn to maneuver large vehicles on crowded streets and in highway traffic. Some programs provide only a limited amount of actual driving experience, and completion of a program does not assure a job. People interested in attending one of these schools should check with local trucking companies to make sure the school's training is acceptable. It is also a good idea to seek a school certified by the Professional Truck Driver Institute of America as providing training that meets Federal Highway Administration guidelines for training tractor-trailer drivers. The Professional Truck Driver Institute of America provides a free list of all their tractor-trailer training programs. Their address is at the end of this chapter.

Training given to new drivers by employers is usually informal, and may consist of only a few hours of instruction from an experienced driver, sometimes on the new employee's own time. New drivers may also ride with and observe experienced drivers before assignment of their own runs. Drivers receive additional training for driving a special type of truck or for handling hazardous materials. Some companies give one to two days of classroom instruction covering general duties, the operation and loading of a truck, company policies, and the preparation of delivery forms and company records. Driver–sales workers also receive training on the various types of products they carry so they will be more effective sales workers and better able to handle customer requests.

Very few people enter truck driving professions directly out of school; most truck drivers previously held jobs in other occupations. Driving experience in the armed forces can be an asset. In some instances, a person may start as a truck driver's helper, driving part of the day and helping to load and unload freight. Senior helpers receive promotions when driving vacancies occur.

New drivers sometimes start on panel or other small "straight" trucks. As they gain experience and show competent driving skills, they may advance to larger and heavier trucks, and finally to tractor-trailers.

Although most new truck drivers are assigned immediately to regular driving jobs, some start as extra drivers, substituting for regular drivers who are ill or on vacation. They receive a regular assignment when an opening occurs.

Advancement of truck drivers is generally limited to driving runs that provide increased earnings or preferred schedules and working conditions. For the most part, a local truck driver may advance to driving heavy or special types of trucks, or transfer to long-distance truck driving. Working for companies that also employ long-distance drivers is the best way to advance to these positions. A few truck drivers may advance to dispatcher, manager, or traffic work—for example, planning delivery schedules.

Some long-distance truck drivers purchase a truck and go into business for themselves. Although many of these owner-operators are successful, some fail to cover expenses and eventually go out of business. Owner-operators should have a good business sense as well as truck driving experience. Courses in accounting, business, and business arithmetic are helpful, and knowledge of truck mechanics can enable owner-operators to perform their own routine maintenance themselves.

JOB OUTLOOK

Truck drivers hold more than three million jobs in North America. Most truck drivers find employment in large metropolitan areas where major trucking, retail, and wholesale companies have their distribution outlets. Some drivers work in rural areas where they provide specialized services, such as delivering milk to dairies or coal to a railhead.

Trucking companies employ about a third of all truck drivers in the United States. Another 30 percent work for companies engaged in wholesale or retail trade, such as auto parts stores, oil companies, lumber yards, or distributors of food and grocery products. The remaining truck drivers are distributed across many industries, including construction, manufacturing, and services.

Fewer than one out of ten truck drivers are self-employed. Of these, a significant number are owner-operators who either serve a variety of businesses independently or lease their services and trucks to a trucking company.

Opportunities should be favorable for people interested in truck driving. This occupation has among the largest number of job openings each year. Although growth in demand for truck drivers will create thousands of openings, the majority will occur as experienced drivers transfer to other fields of work, retire, or leave the labor force for other reasons. Jobs vary greatly in terms of earnings, weekly work hours, number of nights spent on the road, and in the quality of equipment operated. Because truck driving does not require education beyond high school, competition is expected for jobs with the most attractive earnings and working conditions.

Employment of truck drivers is expected to increase about as fast as the average for all occupations through 2006 as the economy grows and the amount of freight carried by trucks increases. The increased use of rail, air, and ship transportation requires truck drivers to pick up and deliver shipments. Growth of long-distance drivers may slow as rail cars increasingly ship loaded trailers across country, but long-distance truck drivers will continue to haul perishable goods.

Average growth of local and long-distance truck driver employment should outweigh the slow growth in driver–sales worker jobs. The number of truck drivers with sales responsibilities is expected to increase slowly because companies are increasingly splitting their responsibilities among other workers. They will shift sales, ordering, and customer service tasks to sales and office staffs, and use regular truck drivers to make deliveries to customers.

Job opportunities may vary from year to year, because the strength of the economy dictates the amount of freight moved by trucks. Companies tend to hire more drivers when the economy is strong and deliveries are in high demand. Consequently, when the economy slows, employers hire fewer drivers or even lay off drivers. Independent owner-operators are particularly vulnerable to slowdowns. Industries least likely to be affected by economic fluctuation tend to be the most stable places for employment.

SALARIES

As a general rule, local truck drivers receive an hourly wage and extra pay for working overtime, usually after forty hours. Employers pay long-distance drivers primarily by the mile. The rate per mile can vary greatly from employer to employer and may even depend on the type of cargo. Typically, earnings increase with mileage driven, seniority, and the size and type of truck driven. Most driver–sales workers receive a commission, based on their sales in addition to an hourly wage.

The average straight-time hourly earnings of truck drivers is about $13.39. Depending on the size of the truck, average hourly earnings are generally as follows:

Medium trucks	$14.64
Tractor-trailers	14.07
Heavy straight trucks	13.17
Light trucks	8.56

Typically, the size of the trucking establishment influences the relative size of drivers' earnings. Drivers employed by large establishments—those with 2,500 or more employees—have the highest earnings. Smaller establishments—those with fewer than 500 employees—have average earnings that range from $8.31 to $16.11 an hour. Truck drivers in the northeast and west have the highest earnings; those in the south have the lowest.

Most long-distance truck drivers operate tractor-trailers, and their earnings vary widely, from as little as $20,000 to over $40,000 annually. Most self-employed truck drivers are primarily engaged in long-distance hauling. After deducting their living expenses and the costs associated with operating their trucks, earnings of $20,000 to $25,000 a year are common.

Many truck drivers are members of the International Brotherhood of Teamsters. Some truck drivers employed by companies outside the trucking industry are members of unions representing the plant workers of the companies for which they work.

RELATED FIELDS

Other driving occupations include ambulance driver, chauffeur, bus driver, and taxi driver.

INTERVIEW
Wally Nickerson
Trucker

Wally Nickerson has been a trucker since 1982. He delivers food for

Kayem Foods in Massachusetts.

How Wally Nickerson Got Started

"What made me pick trucking? I was helping out my brother at Logan Airport doing a part-time job, nights. He is the one who suggested getting my license, so I went for it. This was not something I planned to do or was around as a kid. As a matter of fact, my dad or mom never even had their licenses. My training was pretty much on-the-job training."

What the Job's Really Like

"I'm what they call a local driver p.u.d (pickup and delivery). I'm allowed to drive only 500 miles in a fifteen-hour work day, and only ten of those hours can be driving. I am also only allowed a sixty-hour work week by federal law.

"I get up most mornings at 4:00 A.M., arrive at work by 5:00 A.M., and do my pretrip inspection, basically walking around the truck and observing anything that might need my attention. Then I am rolling by 5:30 A.M.

"Most days my route takes me from Massachusetts to Rhode Island. On an average day I have twelve stops. Some days I drive a forty-two-foot trailer, other days I have up to forty-eight feet to pull.

"Most of the time I deliver full pallets of processed meat (deli).

"It's an interesting job, meeting all kinds of working people. Most are very friendly, that's because I treat them like I would like to be treated.

"I'm usually done with deliveries by 2:00 P.M. That's when I pull over in a safe area with other trucks to rest for a half hour. I usually get home by 5:00 P.M.

"I like the money the job pays. I make $15.50 an hour with full medical and dental insurance. I usually gross about $1,000 a week. I also like my independence on the job. I don't have to answer to anybody most of the day.

"I don't like the weather most of the time in the winter. And I don't like being far from home. I have a young family and that sometimes makes the work stressful, being away from home."

Expert Advice

"Find a company with the right size of trucks you want to drive. When you apply, ask them if training you on the job is an option. If not, go to tractor-trailer school. There are many schools out there. The tuition is about $5,000, and it's worth it.

"The type of person who will do well driving these machines is someone who is patient and drug-free. If you like to party often, you should choose another job."

FOR MORE INFORMATION

Information on truck driver employment opportunities is available from local trucking companies and local offices of the state employment service.

Information on career opportunities in truck driving may be obtained from:

American Trucking Associations, Inc.
2200 Mill Road
Alexandria, VA 22314

American Trucking Association Foundation
660 Roosevelt Avenue
Pawtucket, RI 02860

The Professional Truck Driver Institute of America, a nonprofit organization established by the trucking industry, manufacturers, and others, certifies truck driver training programs meeting industry standards. A free list of certified tractor-trailer driver training programs may be obtained from:

Professional Truck Driver Institute of America
2200 Mill Road
Alexandria, VA 22314

CHAPTER 4

Material-Moving Equipment Operators

EDUCATION
H.S. preferred

$$$ SALARY/EARNINGS
$14,000 to $42,000

OVERVIEW

Material-moving equipment operators use machinery to move construction materials, earth, petroleum products, coal, grain, manufactured goods, and other heavy materials. Generally, they move materials over short distances—around a construction site, factory, warehouse—or on or off trucks and ships.

Operators control equipment by moving levers or foot pedals, operating switches, or turning dials. They may also set up and inspect equipment, make adjustments, and perform minor repairs.

Material-moving equipment operators are classified by the type of equipment they operate. Each piece of equipment requires different skills to move the different types of loads.

Crane and tower operators lift materials, machinery, or other heavy objects from the ground. They extend or retract a horizontally mounted boom to lower or raise a hook attached to the loadline, often in response to hand signals and radioed instructions. Operators position the loads from the on-board console or from a remote console at the site.

While crane and tower operators are conspicuous at office building and other construction sites, the biggest group works in primary metal, metal fabrication, and transportation equipment manufacturing industries that use heavy, bulky materials as inputs.

Excavation and loading machine operators dig and load sand, gravel, earth, or similar materials into trucks or onto conveyors using machinery equipped with scoops, shovels, or buckets. Construction and mining industries employ virtually all excavation and loading machine operators.

Grader, dozer, and scraper operators gouge out, distribute, level, and grade earth with vehicles equipped with a concave blade attached across the front. In addition to the familiar bulldozers, they operate trench excavators, road graders, and similar equipment. Operators maneuver the equipment in successive passes to raise or lower terrain to a specific grade. They may uproot trees and move large rocks while preparing the surface. Although most work in the mining and construction industries, a significant number of grader, dozer, and scraper operators work for state and local governments.

Hoist and winch operators control movement of cables, cages, and platforms to move workers and materials for construction, manufacturing, logging, and other industrial operations. They also lube and maintain the drum and cables and make other minor repairs.

Industrial truck and tractor operators drive and control industrial trucks or tractors equipped with lifting devices, such as a forklift or boom, and trailer hitches. A typical industrial truck, often called a forklift or lift truck, has a hydraulic lifting mechanism and forks. Industrial truck operators use these to carry loads on a skid, or pallet, around a factory or warehouse. They also pull trailers loaded with materials, goods, or equipment within factories and warehouses, or around outdoor storage areas.

Operating engineers are unique in that they use several types of moving equipment. They also may operate and maintain compressors, pumps, and other power equipment at the work site.

Other material-moving equipment operators only tend air compressors or pumps at construction sites, or operate oil or natural gas pumps and compressors at wells and on pipelines. Still, some others operate ship-loading and unloading equipment, conveyors, hoists, and other kinds of various specialized material-handling equipment such as mine or railroad tank car unloading equipment.

Material-moving equipment operators may keep records of materials moved, and do some manual loading and unloading. They also may clean, fuel, and service their equipment.

Many material-moving equipment operators work outdoors, in nearly every type of climate and weather condition. Industrial truck and tractor operators work mainly indoors, in warehouses or manufacturing plants.

Some machines, particularly bulldozers and scrapers, are noisy and shake or jolt the operator. These jobs have become much safer with the adoption of overhead guards on forklift trucks and roll bars on construction machinery. As with most machinery, most accidents can be avoided when observing proper operating procedures and safety practices.

TRAINING

Material-moving equipment operators usually learn their skills on the job. Operators need a good sense of balance, the ability to judge distance, and good eye-hand-foot coordination. Employers of material-moving equipment operators prefer high school graduates, although some equipment may require less education to operate. Mechanical aptitude and high school training in automobile mechanics are helpful because workers may perform some maintenance on their machines. Experience operating mobile equipment, such as farm tractors or heavy equipment in the armed forces, is an asset.

Beginning material-moving equipment operators handle light equipment under the guidance of an experienced operator. Later, they may operate heavier equipment such as bulldozers and cranes. Some construction equipment operators, however, train in formal three-year apprenticeship programs administered by union-management committees of the International Union of Operating Engineers and the Associated General Contractors of America. Because apprentices learn to operate a wider variety of machines than other beginners, they usually have better job opportunities. Apprenticeship programs consist of at least three years, or 6,000 hours of on-the-job training, and 144 hours a year of related classroom instruction.

Private vocational schools offer instruction in the operation of certain types of construction equipment. Completion of such a program may help a person get a job as a trainee or apprentice. However, people considering such training should check the reputation of the school among employers in the area.

JOB OUTLOOK

Material-moving equipment operators hold more than one million jobs nationwide. They are distributed among the detailed occupation groups as follows:

Industrial truck and tractor operators	479,000
Operating engineers	157,000
Grader, dozer, and scraper operators	107,000
Excavation and loading machine operators	97,000
Crane and tower operators	45,000
Hoist and winch operators	9,000
All other material-moving equipment operators	202,000

The largest proportion—30 percent—of material-moving equipment operators work in manufacturing. Most of these are industrial truck and tractor operators or crane and tower operators; a little over 50 percent of both work for manufacturing companies.

More than 25 percent of all material-moving equipment operators work in mining and construction; these operators are mostly in the remaining occupations, nearly half of whom work in these two industries.

Significant numbers of industrial truck and tractor operators also work in state and local governments and in the trucking and warehousing, and wholesale trade industries. State and local governments also employ a large proportion of grader, dozer, and scraper operators and operating engineers. A few material-moving equipment operators are self-employed.

Material-moving equipment operators work in every section of the country. Some work in remote locations on large construction projects, such as highways and dams, or in factory or mining operations.

Employment of material-moving equipment operators will increase about as fast as the average for all occupations through 2006. The expected growth stems from increased spending on improving the nation's infrastructure of highways, bridges, and dams. However, equipment improvements, including the growing automation of material handling in factories and warehouses, continue to raise productivity and moderate demand for skilled operators.

In addition to employment growth in this large occupation, many jobs will open up because of the need to replace experienced workers who transfer to other occupations or leave the labor force.

Growth of employment among material-moving equipment operators largely depends on the growth of the various industries that employ them. Construction and manufacturing employ the majority of these workers.

Total employment in construction will grow more slowly than the average for all occupations, but employment of material-moving equipment operators in construction will grow as fast as the average. Employment of operators in manufacturing should decline in tandem with overall industry employment. However, very rapid employment growth of material-moving operators is expected in temporary help organizations and companies that lease equipment.

Growth of industrial truck and tractor operators, the largest occupation in this group, will be about as fast as the average for all occupations because of increased demand for operators who can maneuver multiple pieces of equipment.

In addition, more operator jobs will result as large factories and warehouses consolidate material-handling systems and require more operators. However, growth of industrial truck and tractor operators will be constrained by technological improvements. Some systems use computerized dispatching or onboard data communication devices to enable industrial truck and tractor operators to move goods more efficiently. In other handling systems, industrial trucks and tractors may be replaced by computer-controlled conveyor systems, overhead handling systems, or automated vehicles that do not require operators.

Precision computerized controls and robotics will automate crane and tower operator and hoist and winch operator positions, slowing employment growth. Slow employment growth in construction and declines in manufacturing should cause all other material-moving equipment operating occupations to grow more slowly than the average for all occupations.

In addition, both construction and manufacturing are very sensitive to changes in economic conditions, so the number of job openings for operators in these industries may fluctuate from year to year.

SALARIES

Earnings for material-moving equipment operators vary considerably. In 1996, median earnings of all material-moving equipment operators were $456 a week; the middle 50 percent earned between $329 and $606. The lowest 10 percent earned an average $264 a week and the highest 10 percent averaged $806 a week.

The following shows 1996 median weekly earnings among the detailed occupation groups:

Crane and tower operators	$551.00
Operating engineers	508.00
Grader, dozer, and scraper operators	490.00
Hoist and winch operators	490.00
Excavation and loading machine operators	485.00
Industrial truck and tractor operators	415.00
All other material-moving equipment operators	451.00

Pay scales generally are higher in large metropolitan areas. Annual earnings of some workers may be lower than weekly rates would indicate, because the amount of time they work may be limited by bad weather.

RELATED FIELDS

Other workers who operate mechanical equipment include truck and bus drivers, manufacturing equipment operators, and farmers.

INTERVIEW
Terry Goodwin
Overhead Crane Operator

Terry Goodwin is an overhead crane operator with Elkem Metals in

Alloy, West Virginia. He has been with them for more than ten years.

How Terry Goodwin Got Started

"What attracted me to this job was operating equipment. I like the controls! After completing my high school education, I received certification for operation and maintenance of heavy equipment through a technical school. Then I had to go through six weeks of on-the-job training."

What the Job's Really Like

"My duties are to lift and pour 100-cubic-feet ladles of molten silicon metal into ingots (chilles). Each chill weighs approximately one ton. After the silicon solidifies, I then lift and transfer it to cooling grids.

"This job never gets boring to me. If anything, it is a challenge. The cab of the crane is about six stories high. I operate both from the cab and from a remote control box at ground level.

"Crane operating at the plant is a good job. A good operator has to have very good hand and eye coordination. If the crane operator is slow or rough, then everyone has a bad shift. He must be steady and smooth in our operation, while handling molten metal.

"I work a forty-hour week as a union hourly worker. My wage scale is $16 per hour, straight time. My yearly income at the plant is about $36,000. With overtime it can be $5,000 to $10,000 a year more. I have great medical coverage also.

"What I like best about my job is operating such a powerful piece of equipment. The crane I operate has two lifting hoists. One has a big thirty-ton capacity and the other has a five-ton capacity. I must always keep them both under control at the same time; they are used simultaneously.

"I also like being able to lift very heavy objects and transfer them with ease. This sometimes amazes me. When I am operating from the cab, I can see every little movement below me.

"Just like in any job, things can go wrong. Sometimes cranes break down—usually when you are right in the middle of making a move. Then I must wait for repair people and hope they can fix it fast enough to keep me on schedule. Most times the cranes run great. Usually I have to operate from a wireless remote control box that I wear on a harness in front of me. The plant converted to these about two years ago. Some people like them and some don't. I am learning to like them.

"Another thing is I have to operate for different people through the work week. It can be different for each person. So, I have to be flexible.

"The only other downside to my job is that it can get pretty hot at work. Molten silicon is about 2,600 to 3,100 degrees Fahrenheit. So it's good to get out of the heat for awhile."

Expert Advice

"If you want to become a crane operator, you should not try to rush through your training. Training is usually provided at the job sites of plants where the equipment is used.

"A crane operator should have acceptable vision; depth perception is a must. An operator should have very good hand and eye coordination and not be afraid of heights.

"Also, operators should have the ability to work safely around people and objects. I am sure that anyone starting a crane operating job will like it."

INTERVIEW
Andy Jones
Bulldozer Operator

Andy Jones is a loader operator for Brandywine Patio, a stoneyard in West Chester, Pennsylvania. He started working in the field during his last year of high school in 1992.

How Andy Jones Got Started

"I always liked working outside. I grew up around backhoes and stuff so I knew how to do it. My dad started my training at first, then I took some classes at a local school.

"I got my job by responding to an ad in the paper."

What the Job's Really Like

"Basically, I drive and load a truck, either with pallets of brick or gravel or stone. I am responsible for keeping the truck road-legal—lights, plates, inspection, tags, tires, etc.—and I also am responsible for one bulldozer and two backhoes, all Deere. If something goes wrong, I have to fix them.

"I'm always busy. There is no end to all the things that need to be done, whether it's a delivery 100 miles away or a footer that needs to be dug.

"I usually work sixty-five to seventy-five-hour weeks and make $12.50 an hour. The atmosphere is far from formal, which I can't say I dislike.

"On the downside, you get dirty at this job and you're always sore at the end of the day. Also, you don't meet many people. When you're pulled into a restaurant and you're eating in the truck, you look up and see a couple walking by. You wonder, 'Shouldn't that be me?' but you realize that trucking stands in the way of your getting lots of chances to meet someone on a friend and girlfriend level.

"But I like being by myself, just listening to the truck engine moaning out its one-note song, just being alone away from everything. It gives you time to think about stuff.

"I also like running the loaders and doing nice work, something I can take pride in. When I'm done, I say that looks good."

Expert Advice

"You have to have lots of patience and never lose your cool and never get out of line with customers. You can't drink, either. If you come in hungover or drunk, you could lose your license for a long time.

"To be a good operator you need training. Many places offer full courses, but most importantly you need loads of experience."

INTERVIEW
John Bisig
Operating Engineer

John Bisig is an operating engineer with ROC Enterprises, Inc., a general contractor specializing in commercial site development, in Maywood, New Jersey. He is dispatched to ROC exclusively through Operating Engineers Local 825. He has been in the construction industry since 1975.

How John Bisig Got Started

"When I was three years old, my father bought me a battery-operated bulldozer for Christmas, and taught me how to tow the coffee table around the living room (honest). As a child I was always in awe of the power and size of heavy construction equipment and would recreate what I saw on job sites with my Tonka toys. This interest only grew, and as I got older, I found out that it paid well, which served to seal my fate.

"I was hired at sixteen years old as a laborer for an asphalt paving contractor. I was taught the duties of laborer on the job and introduced to operating paving equipment shortly thereafter. I had eight weeks of formal schooling while on active duty in the U.S. Navy, but 99 percent of what I know I learned in the field.

"I got my current job because of my affiliation with the union. When a union contractor needs an equipment operator, he calls the operating engineers union hall and requests an operator according to the skills required for that particular position. The dispatcher reviews the out-of-work list, and picks the first qualified operator in line and dispatches him or her to that job. However, once an operator has worked for a particular contractor, that contractor may make a specific request for that operator, as was the case with me. ROC had a standing request for me."

What the Job's Really Like

"My job consists solely of operating heavy construction equipment in all the different phases and operations required for commercial site development. I have also worked in highway construction, pipeline, demolition, clearing, earthwork, landscaping, bridge building, quarry operation, paving, hazardous material remediation, and materials handling.

"Learning all the different disciplines is not required; many operators are proficient in only one or two, which is sufficient to be on the same pay scale as I am. I work exclusively through the International Union of Operating Engineers—Local 825. By way of our collective bargaining agreement, we are paid the prevailing wage for the state of New Jersey. Journeymen rates range from $40 to $44 an hour, with a few variables of a dollar or two for long boom crane operators or lead engineers. We are also guaranteed forty hours a week minimum. Anything over eight hours in a day is at time and a half, all day Saturday is time and a half, and Sunday is double time. There are seven paid holidays. There is also a four-year apprentice program available that pays from 65 percent to 85 percent of the journeyman rate. Operators who work nonunion can expect to be paid from $12 to $18 an hour, depending on experience. However if they work on a tax-funded project, the law mandates they are to be paid the prevailing union wage scale.

"My workday starts at 7:00 A.M. I operate a Caterpillar 350 series excavator, which is a digging machine weighing thirty-five metric tons. My duties are to separate, consolidate, and load onto off-road dump trucks excess materials that are on the forty-acre site we are developing. This is to establish a fairly level plane in preparation for excavation operations to begin.

"As an operating engineer, it is my duty to check my machine before each day begins. I must check all oil levels and fuel level, grease all points and attachments, and inspect the general condition of the machine. During my shift I will monitor all gauges, and periodically inspect the condition of the machine's systems.

"I am also responsible for operating the machine in a manner that ensures the safety of my coworkers, myself, and the equipment.

"I also control the loading operation itself. I must establish where I will position my machine and where the trucks will line up to be loaded, productivity and ease of operation being the determining factors. Once I establish this, I will load materials until I exhaust that pile, then move to the next one and repeat the procedure. The pace at which the operation moves is determined by how many trucks are being loaded and how far they must travel. Some days I have only one truck to load, which gives me a lull in between loads; other days I have several trucks, which keeps me loading one after another nonstop.

"Loading trucks is only one of the many different operations I'll perform during the course of this project. Last week I was operating a Caterpillar D5H-LGP bulldozer, doing precision grading of the stone base in a 130,000-square-foot building, preparing for the masons to pour the concrete floor. This type of operation has a much greater degree of difficulty, and requires much more experience on the part of the operator. Only about 10 percent of the operators in the industry can perform this type of work productively.

"The equipment used here is state-of-the-art, and the finish is checked by laser. Adding to the degree of difficulty is the fact that there are usually other trades—masons, ironworkers, carpenters—working in and around the building, making safety of paramount importance. There's much more to this craft than just climbing into a machine and pulling levers, which for me, keeps it interesting and ever-changing, besides being lots of fun. And who hasn't driven past a construction site and wondered what it would be like to operate one of those huge machines?

"Some of the most rewarding aspects of my profession are the completions. I'm never in the same place for very long; we do the project from start to finish, then move to the next project, leaving in our path a succession of huge masterpieces that will stand for years to come.

"As a highly experienced operator, I don't do the same thing day-in and day-out. I operate a wide variety of machines in a wide variety of operations, across a wide variety of disciplines. And, yes it is fun to operate those huge machines!

"The downside to being an operator is exposure to inclement weather conditions, dust, noise, and the inherent danger—all of which can be minimized with proper gear and education, but never eliminated.

"The other downside is that the amount of work in the industry is directly influenced by the state of the economy."

Expert Advice

"Almost no contractor will hire an operator with no experience because of the danger involved. There are private trade schools for equipment operators, union apprenticeship programs, and the military as sources of formal training. Some companies may even train operators, depending on their need.

"It takes thousands of hours of field experience to become a top-notch operator, and you must possess certain natural abilities such as, depth perception, ambidextrous coordination, mechanical aptitude, and a will to learn. A working knowledge of geometry helps, too."

FOR MORE INFORMATION

For further information about apprenticeships or work opportunities for construction equipment operators, contact a local of the International Union of Operating Engineers; a local apprenticeship committee; or the nearest office of the state apprenticeship agency.

In addition, the local office of the state employment service may provide information about apprenticeship and other training programs.

For general information about the work of construction equipment operators, contact:

National Center for Construction Education and Research
University of Florida
P.O. Box 141104
Gainesville, FL 32614-1104

Associated General Contractors of America, Inc.
1957 E Street NW
Washington, DC 20006

International Union of Operating Engineers
1125 17th Street NW
Washington, DC 20036

Specialized Carriers and Rigging Association
2750 Prosperity Avenue, Suite 620
Fairfax, VA 22301

Information on industrial truck and tractor operators is available from:

Industrial Truck Association
1750 K Street NW, Suite 460
Washington, DC 20006

CHAPTER **5** Water Transportation Occupations

🎓 **EDUCATION**
H.S. preferred

💲💲💲 **SALARY/EARNINGS**
$15,000 to $60,000

OVERVIEW

Workers in water transportation occupations operate and maintain deep sea merchant ships, tugboats, towboats, ferries, dredges, research vessels, and other waterborne craft on the oceans and the Great Lakes, in harbors, on rivers and canals, and on other waterways.

Captains or masters are in overall command of the operation of a vessel and they supervise the work of the other officers and the crew. They set course and speed, maneuver the vessel to avoid hazards and other ships, and periodically determine position using navigation aids, celestial observations, and charts. They direct crew members who steer the vessel, operate engines, signal to other vessels, perform maintenance and handle lines, or operate towing or dredging gear. Captains ensure that proper procedures and safety practices are followed, check that machinery and equipment are in good working order, and oversee the loading and unloading of cargo or passengers. They also maintain logs and other records of ships' movements and cargo carried.

Captains on large vessels are assisted by deck officers or mates. Merchant marine vessels—those carrying cargo overseas—have a chief or first mate, a second mate, and a third mate. Mates oversee the operation of the vessel, or "stand watch" for specified periods, usually four hours on and eight hours off. On smaller vessels, there may be only one mate (called a pilot on some inland vessels) who alternates watches with the captain.

Engineers or marine engineers operate, maintain, and repair propulsion engines, boilers, generators, pumps, and other machinery. Merchant marine vessels usually have four engineering officers: a chief engineer and a first, second, and third assistant engineer. Assistant engineers stand periodic watches, overseeing the operation of engines and machinery.

Seamen, also called deckhands, particularly on inland waters, operate the vessel and its deck equipment under the direction of the ship's officers, and keep the nonengineering areas in good condition. They stand watch, looking out for other vessels, obstructions in the ship's path, and aids to navigation. They also steer the ship, measure water depth in shallow water, and maintain and operate deck equipment such as life boats, anchors, and cargo-handling gear. When docking or departing, they handle lines. They also perform maintenance chores such as repairing lines, chipping rust, and painting and cleaning decks and other areas. Seamen may also load and unload cargo. On vessels handling liquid cargo, they hook up hoses, operate pumps, and clean tanks. Deckhands on tugboats or tow vessels tie barges together into tow units, inspect them periodically, and disconnect them when the destination is reached. Larger vessels have a boatswain or head seaman.

Marine oilers work below decks under the direction of the ship's engineers. They lubricate gears, shafts, bearings, and other moving parts of engines and motors, read pressure and temperature gauges and record data, and may repair and adjust machinery.

A typical deep sea merchant ship has a captain, three deck officers or mates, a chief engineer and three assistant engineers, plus six or more seamen and oilers. Depending on their size, vessels operating in harbors, rivers, or along the coast may have a crew comprising only a captain and one deckhand, or as many as a captain, a mate or pilot, an engineer, and seven or eight seamen. Large vessels also have a full-time cook and helper, while on small ones, a seaman does the cooking. Merchant ships also have an electrician, machinery mechanics, and a radio officer.

Pilots guide ships in and out of harbors, through straits, and on rivers and other confined waterways where a familiarity with local water depths, winds, tides, currents, and hazards such as reefs and shoals is of prime importance. Pilots on river and canal vessels usually are regular crew members, like mates. Harbor pilots are generally independent contractors, who accompany vessels while they enter or leave port. They may pilot many ships in a single day.

Merchant mariners are away from home for extended periods, but earn long leaves. Most are hired for one voyage, with no job security after that. At sea, they usually stand watch for four hours and are off for eight hours, seven days a week. Those employed on Great Lakes ships work sixty days and have thirty days off, but do not work in the winter when the lakes are frozen over. Workers on rivers and canals and in harbors are more likely to have year-round work. Some work eight- or twelve-hour shifts and go home every day. Others work steadily for a week or month and then have an extended period off. When working, they are usually on duty for six or twelve hours and are off for six or twelve hours.

People in water transportation occupations work in all weather conditions, and although merchant mariners try to avoid severe storms while at sea, working in damp and cold conditions is unpleasant. It is uncommon for vessels to sink, but workers nevertheless face the possibility that they may have to abandon their craft on short notice if it collides with other vessels or runs aground. They also risk injury or death from falling overboard and hazards associated with working with machinery, heavy loads, and dangerous cargo.

Some newer vessels are air-conditioned, soundproofed from noisy machinery, and have comfortable living quarters. Nevertheless, some workers do not like the long periods away from home and the confinement aboard ship.

TRAINING

Entry, training, and educational requirements for most water transportation occupations are established and regulated by the U.S. Coast Guard. All officers and operators of watercraft must be licensed by the U.S. Coast Guard, which offers nearly sixty different licenses, depending on the position and type of craft. Licensing differs somewhat between the merchant marine and others.

Deck and engineering officers in the merchant marine must be licensed. To qualify for a license, applicants must have graduated from the U.S. Merchant Marine Academy, or one of the six state academies, and pass a written examination. A physical examination and a drug test are also required. People with at least three years of appropriate sea experience also can be licensed if they pass the written exam, but it is difficult to pass without substantial formal schooling or independent study. Also, because seamen may work six months a year or less, it can take from five to eight years to accumulate the necessary experience.

The academies offer four-year bachelor's degree programs (one offers a three-year associate program) in nautical science or marine engineering to prepare students to be third mates or third assistant engineers. With experience and passing of additional exams, third officers may qualify for higher rank. Because of keen competition, however, officers may have to take jobs below the grade for which they are qualified.

For employment in the merchant marine as an unlicensed seaman, a merchant mariner's document is needed. Applicants for merchant marine documents do not need to be U.S. citizens. A medical certificate of excellent health, and a certificate attesting to vision, color perception, and general physical condition may be required for higher-level deckhands. While no experience or formal schooling is required, training at a union-operated school is helpful. Beginners are classified as Ordinary Seamen and may be assigned to the deck or engineering department. With experience at sea, and perhaps union-sponsored training, an ordinary seaman can pass the able seaman exam.

Merchant marine officers and seamen, both experienced and beginners, are hired for voyages through union hiring halls or directly by shipping companies.

Harbor pilot training is usually an apprenticeship with a shipping company or a pilot employees' association. Entrants may be able seamen or licensed officers.

No training or experience is needed to become a seaman or deckhand on vessels operating in harbors or on rivers or other waterways. Newly hired workers generally learn skills on the job. With experience, they are eligible to take a coast guard exam to qualify as a mate, pilot, or captain. Substantial knowledge gained through experience, courses in seamanship schools, and independent study are needed to pass the exam.

JOB OUTLOOK

Water transportation workers held about 51,000 jobs in 1996. The total number who worked during some point in the year was somewhat higher because many merchant marine officers and seamen worked only part of the year. The following tabulation shows employment in the occupations that make up this group:

Ship captains and mates	21,000
Sailors and deckhands	22,000
Marine engineers	9,000

Over 1,400 of the captains and pilots were self-employed, operating their own vessel, or were pilots who were independent contractors.

About 40 percent of all water transportation workers were employed on board merchant marine ships or U.S. Navy Military Sealift ships operating on the oceans or Great Lakes. Another 40 percent were employed in transportation services, working on tugs, towboats, ferries, dredges, and other watercraft in harbors, on rivers and canals, and other waterways.

Others worked in water transportation services such as piloting vessels in and out of harbors, operating lighters and chartered boats, and in marine construction, salvaging, and surveying. The remaining water transportation workers were employed on vessels that carry passengers, such as cruise ships, casino boats, sightseeing and excursion boats, and ferries.

Keen competition is expected to continue for jobs in water transportation occupations. Overall, employment in water transportation occupations is projected to decline through 2006. Opportunities will vary by sector.

Employment in deep sea shipping is expected to continue its long-term sharp decline as U.S.-staffed ships carry an even smaller proportion of international cargo. Stringent federal regulations require larger crews on U.S.-flagged ships, which allow vessels that fly foreign flags and have smaller crew sizes to operate at lower cost and make a larger profit. A fleet of deep sea U.S.-flagged ships is considered to be vital to the nation's defense, so some receive federal support through a maritime security subsidy and other provisions in laws limit certain federal cargoes to ships that fly the U.S. flag.

Newer ships are designed to be operated safely by much smaller crews. Innovations include automated controls and computerized monitoring systems in navigation, engine control, watchkeeping, ship management, and cargo handling. As older vessels are replaced, crew responsibilities will change. Seamen will need to learn new skills to be able to handle these varied duties.

Vessels on rivers and canals and on the Great Lakes carry mostly bulk products such as coal, iron ore, petroleum, sand and gravel, grain, and chemicals. Shipments of these products are expected to grow through 2006, but productivity increases should cause employment to decline. Employment in water transportation services is likely to show little or no change.

The decline in new opportunities has created competition for existing jobs, with many experienced merchant mariners going for long periods without work. As a result, unions generally accept few new members. Also, many Merchant Marine Academy graduates have not found licensed shipboard jobs in the U.S. Merchant Marine, although most do find industry-related jobs. Most are commissioned as ensigns in the U.S. Naval Reserve, and some may be selected for active duty in the navy. Some find jobs as seamen on U.S.-flagged or foreign-flagged vessels, tugboats, other watercraft, or civilian jobs with the U.S. Navy. Some take land-based jobs with shipping companies, marine insurance companies, manufacturers of boilers or related machinery, or other related jobs. Unless the number of people seeking merchant marine jobs declines sharply, the present intense competition is likely to continue.

SALARIES

Water transportation workers who usually worked full-time had median weekly earnings of $579 in 1996. The middle 50 percent earned between $402 and $860 a week. The lowest 10 percent earned less than $287, while the highest 10 percent earned more than $1,157 a week.

Captains and mates had median weekly earnings of $653 a week in 1996. The middle 50 percent earned between $394 and $904 a week. The lowest paid 10 percent earned less than $275, while the highest earned more than $1,203 a week.

Seamen had median weekly earnings of $520 a week in 1996. The middle 50 percent earned between $395 and $695 a week. The lowest 10 percent earned less than $288 a week, while the highest 10 percent earned more than $983 a week.

RELATED FIELDS

Workers in occupations having duties and responsibilities similar to these occupations include fishing vessel captains, ferryboat operators, and long shoremen.

INTERVIEW
Thomas MacPherson
Chief Engineer

Thomas MacPherson has had fourteen years sea time in the U.S. Navy and one year with Edison Chouest Offshore, an offshore support enterprise in Galiano, Louisiana.

How Thomas MacPherson Got Started

"I was in the navy for eighteen years, and retired early, just over a year ago. I chose joining the navy to leave the area I grew up in (McKeesport, Pennsylvania) because the steel industry was dying out and I wanted to see something different. My father and older brother were in the navy as well.

"The job I am doing now is similar to what I knew in the navy, although less intense and more informal—a lot more fun."

What the Job's Really Like

"The type of boat I work on is an elevator support ship. My company's primary role is support of the oil industry by transporting crews and supplies to and from the oil rigs. We also transport what is called liquid mud—for pumping into the oil wells to displace the oil.

"My present position is chief engineer, and my duties are to supervise and operate the engine room and various engineering aspects of the boat. Log keeping, engine operation, fuel, water, electricity, and some electronics are required to be operated or maintained. For example, today I operated the diesel engines, worked on the phone lines, helped with the deck hands in a small boat, and operated the hydraulic system to lower the submarine elevator system.

"My company does a lot of work with various navy projects, such as submarine testing and even the recovery of the U.S.S. *Monitor* propeller and shaft from off the coast of North Carolina.

"The most enjoyable part of the job is the maintenance and operation of the boats. I like to learn something new every day and it's nice to get to work on something different from time to time. As long as it is done safely and correctly, there are very few things you can't do.

"The downside is the time that is spent away from home—but I actually enjoy going out to sea, getting away for a time to catch up on reading or movies. The pay is good and it does provide food and a bunk. The pay is based on a day rate. Starting out as an oiler, $85 to $120 is normal. An assistant engineer can make from $150 to $200 a day. A chief engineer from $200-plus a day. It depends on your license, the company, the work location, and the boat contract."

Expert Advice

"The qualities you should have include dependability, responsibility, patience, and most importantly, you shouldn't be afraid of hard work.

"It is possible to shorten some requirements by attending one of the merchant marine academies, but for my case the U.S. Navy provided me with the prerequisites for my present license. Coast guard or navy sea time are partially credited toward merchant marine sea time.

"For the offshore vessel work I am in, knowledge of diesels is a prerequisite. For ocean vessels, steam and/or diesel knowledge is necessary. In both cases, electrical and fluid system knowledge are required.

"As for starting out, sea time is sea time. Whether going to the Gulf of Mexico (Louisiana and Texas), Alaska, or even to the Northeast—Massachusetts or Rhode Island—for the fishing fleet, all require some seagoing experience to get into the job.

"A lot of junior engineers start out as Ordinary Seamen (OS). Or you can start out in the seagoing services (navy or coast guard) as I did."

INTERVIEW
Richard Turnwald
Cruise Ship Purser

Richard Turnwald has been working in the cruise industry for more than fourteen years. He started out shoreside, in the operations department where he handled everything from personnel to ordering supplies for the ships. He went from there to positions with the cruise staff as a shore excursions director, assistant cruise director, and port lecturer providing information on the different ports-of-call. He then worked his way up the ranks from junior purser to chief purser.

How Richard Turnwald Got Started

"Ever since I was a little boy I've always loved ships and the sea. I read about them and studied them and there was no doubt in my mind that I wanted to be involved in some way with ships as a profession.

"I was in college in Michigan studying travel and tourism and I wanted to get involved with the cruise lines. I sent out my resume and wrote to the various cruise lines, most of which were based in Miami. I was interviewed over the telephone and was offered a position in the office. It was exciting and scary at the same time. I was just out of college and I had to relocate to a place where I didn't know anyone, but it was like a dream for me to finally be able to work closely with the cruise ships."

What the Job's Really Like

"The purser's office is like the front desk at a big hotel. The staff handle all the money on the ship, they pay all the bills and the salaries, they cash traveler's checks for passengers, provide the safes for the valuables, fill out all the documentation for customs and immigration officials in the different countries, and all the other crucial behind-the-scenes functions.

"The purser is who passengers come to for information or help with problems. Pursers are in charge of cabin assignments, and they also coordinate with the medical personnel to help handle any emergencies.

"There are various ranks for a purser: junior or assistant purser, second purser, first purser, then chief purser. As chief purser I had a staff of six people I was responsible for; on larger ships the purser's office might have fourteen or fifteen people.

"Promotions are based on your ability, how well you do your job, as well as the length of time you've been employed. I was fortunate, I rose up through the ranks fairly quickly. Within three months I had worked my way up from junior purser to chief purser. But that's really an exceptional situation. It usually takes a good year or so. It depends on how many people are ahead of you, if they leave or stay.

"It can be competitive. You have to consider that there's only one chief purser on each ship. Some people start working on a ship and their only background was watching *The Love Boat* and thinking from that how wonderful it would be. They don't have a realistic viewpoint of the downsides of cruise work.

"When you live and work on a ship, you're an employee, you're not there to be a passenger. The living conditions are not as luxurious as for the passengers, you might be sharing a room with one or two other crew members, and there's not a lot of privacy. There's a sense of confinement on a ship; you can't just go out to dinner whenever you want. Experiencing cabin fever is common. You live your job twenty-four hours a day and there's no getting away from that.

"The food isn't as high class; passengers might be having lobster and steak upstairs; the crew is eating fish or meatloaf below. You might be away from home for the first time and feeling homesick and cut off. When you work on a ship you're on duty seven days a week, you don't have a day off for several months at a time. Some people can get burned out on that, while others can thrive.

"If you take a positive approach, you realize that you don't have to commute to work or worry about housing. Though you don't get an entire day off, you get several hours at a time when you're in port and you get to see a lot of wonderful things. I've been all over the world, to places I wouldn't have had the time or money to get to otherwise. I've been to the Caribbean, Alaska, South America, Antarctica, Europe, and Hawaii. If you're on an itinerary that repeats every week, you get to know that place very well and the people there, so that's a plus.

"And there's something so relaxing and peaceful about being at sea, just to stand by the railing of the deck and see the changes in the weather and the whales and the other sealife. Another advantage is the money. You work hard and very intensely for long periods of time, but typically you're paid very well and it's a good opportunity to save money. I was able to buy a house."

Expert Advice

"Work on people skills: be friendly, be helpful, and be courteous. It's very important—you'll be representing the cruise line to a lot of people.

"And you have to be willing and able to accept orders. It isn't as strict as the navy, but when you're on a ship there are many rules and guidelines you have to follow. You've heard the expression, 'to run a tight ship' . . . you have to have regulations to do that. If you're too independent-minded and don't like to be told what to do, then ship life wouldn't be for you."

FOR MORE INFORMATION

Information on merchant marine careers, training, and licensing requirements is available from:

Maritime Administration
U.S. Department of Transportation
400 7th Street SW, Room 302
Washington, DC 20590

U.S. Coast Guard
Licensing and Manning Compliance Division (C-MOC-1)
2100 2nd Street, SW
Washington, DC 20593-0001

Individuals interested in attending a merchant marine academy should contact:

Admissions Office
U.S. Merchant Marine Academy
Steamboat Road
Kings Point, NY 11024

To find out more about working for a cruise line contact:

Cruise Line International Association
500 5th Avenue, Suite 1407
New York, NY 10110

CHAPTER 6 Aviation Occupations

OVERVIEW

Aircraft Pilots

EDUCATION
B.A./B.S. preferred

$$$ SALARY/EARNINGS
$15,000 to $200,000

Pilots are highly trained professionals who fly airplanes and helicopters to carry out a wide variety of tasks. Although most pilots transport passengers and cargo, others are involved in more unusual tasks, such as dusting crops, spreading seed for reforestation, testing aircraft, directing firefighting efforts, tracking criminals, monitoring traffic, and rescuing and evacuating injured persons. The vast majority of pilots fly airplanes.

Except on small aircraft, two pilots usually make up the cockpit crew. Generally, the most experienced pilot (called captain) is in command and supervises all other crew members. The copilot assists in communicating with air traffic controllers, monitoring the instruments, and flying the aircraft. Some large aircraft still have a third pilot in the cockpit, the flight engineer, who assists the other pilots by monitoring and operating many of the instruments and systems, making minor in-flight repairs, and watching for other aircraft. New technology can perform many flight tasks, however, and virtually all new aircraft now fly with only two pilots, who rely more heavily on computerized controls.

Before departure, pilots plan their flights carefully. They thoroughly check their aircraft to make sure that the engines, controls, instruments, and other systems are functioning properly.

They also make sure that the baggage and cargo have been loaded correctly. They confer with flight dispatchers and aviation weather forecasters to find out about weather conditions enroute and at their destination. Based on this information, they choose a route, altitude, and speed that should provide the fastest, safest, and smoothest flight. When flying under instrument flight rules (procedures governing the operation of the aircraft when there is poor visibility), the pilot in command or the company dispatcher normally files an instrument flight plan with air traffic control so that the flight can be coordinated with other air traffic.

Takeoff and landing are the most difficult parts of the flight and require close coordination between the pilot and copilot. For example, as the plane accelerates for takeoff, the pilot concentrates on the runway while the copilot scans the instrument panel. To calculate the speed they must attain to become airborne, pilots consider the altitude of the airport, outside temperature, weight of the plane, and the speed and direction of the wind. The moment the plane reaches takeoff speed, the copilot informs the pilot, who then pulls back on the controls to raise the nose of the plane.

Unless the weather is bad, the actual flight is relatively easy. Airplane pilots, with the assistance of autopilot and the flight management computer, steer the plane along their planned route and are monitored by the air traffic control stations they pass along the way. They continuously scan the instrument panel to check their fuel supply, the condition of their engines, and the air-conditioning, hydraulic, and other systems. Pilots may request a change in altitude or route if circumstances dictate. For example, if the ride is rougher than expected, they may ask air traffic control if pilots flying at other altitudes have reported better conditions. If so, they may request a change. This procedure also may be used to find a stronger tailwind or a weaker headwind to save fuel and increase speed.

Because helicopters are used for short trips at relatively low altitude, pilots must be constantly on the lookout for trees, bridges, power lines, transmission towers, and other dangerous obstacles. Regardless of the type of aircraft, all pilots must monitor warning devices designed to help detect sudden shifts in wind conditions that can cause crashes.

If visibility is poor, pilots must rely completely on their instruments. Using the altimeter readings, they know how high above ground they are and whether or not they can fly safely over mountains and other obstacles. Special navigation radios give pilots precise information which, with the help of special maps, tell them their exact position. Other very sophisticated equipment provides directions to a point just above the end of a runway and enables pilots to land completely blind.

Once on the ground, pilots must complete records on their flight for their organization and the Federal Aviation Administration (FAA).

The number of nonflying duties that pilots have depends on the employment setting. Airline pilots have the services of large support staffs and consequently perform few nonflying duties. Pilots employed by other organizations such as charters or business operators have many other duties. They may load the aircraft, handle all passenger luggage to ensure a balanced load, and supervise refueling; other nonflying responsibilities include keeping records, scheduling flights, arranging for major maintenance, and performing minor maintenance and repair work on their aircraft.

Some pilots are instructors. They teach their students the principles of flight in ground-school classes and demonstrate how to operate aircraft in dual-controlled planes and helicopters. A few specially trained pilots are examiners or check pilots. They periodically fly with other pilots or applicants to make sure that they are proficient.

EDUCATION
H.S. preferred

SALARY/EARNINGS
$12,000 to $40,000

Flight Attendants

It is the job of the flight attendant to see that all passengers have a safe, comfortable, and enjoyable flight. At least one hour before each flight, attendants are briefed by the captain on such things as expected weather conditions and special passenger problems. The attendants see that the passenger cabin is in order, that supplies of food, beverages, blankets, and reading material are adequate, and that first-aid kits and other emergency equipment are aboard and in working order. As passengers board the plane, attendants greet them, check their tickets, and assist them in storing coats and carry-on luggage.

Before the plane takes off, attendants instruct passengers in the use of emergency equipment and check to see that all passengers have their seat belts fastened and seat backs forward. In the air, they answer questions about the flight; distribute reading material, pillows, and blankets; and help care for small children, elderly, and disabled persons. They may administer first aid to passengers who become ill. Attendants also serve cocktails and other refreshments and, on many flights, heat and distribute precooked meals. After the plane has landed, flight attendants assist passengers as they leave the plane. They then prepare reports on medications given to passengers, lost and found articles, and cabin equipment conditions. Some flight attendants straighten up the plane's cabin.

Helping passengers in the event of an emergency is the most important responsibility of the flight attendant. This may range from reassuring passengers during occasional encounters with strong turbulence to directing passengers in evacuating a plane following an emergency landing.

Lead or first flight attendants aboard planes oversee the work of the other attendants while performing most of the same duties.

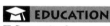

EDUCATION
H.S. required

$$$ SALARY/EARNINGS
$30,000 to $60,000

Air Traffic Controllers

The air traffic control system is a vast network of people and equipment that ensures the safe operation of commercial and private aircraft. Air traffic controllers coordinate the movement of air traffic to make certain that planes stay a safe distance apart. Their immediate concern is safety, but controllers also must direct planes efficiently to minimize delays. Some regulate airport traffic; others regulate flights between airports.

Although airport tower or terminal controllers watch over all planes traveling through the airport's airspace, their main responsibility is to organize the flow of aircraft in and out of the airport. Relying on radar and visual observation, they closely monitor each plane to ensure a safe distance between all aircraft and to guide pilots between the hangar or ramp and the end of the airport's airspace. In addition, controllers keep pilots informed about changes in weather conditions such as wind shear, a sudden change in the velocity or direction of the wind that can cause the pilot to lose control of the aircraft.

During arrival or departure, several controllers handle each plane. As a plane approaches an airport, the pilot radios ahead to inform the terminal of its presence. The controller in the radar room just beneath the control tower has a copy of the plane's flight plan and already has observed the plane on radar. If the way is clear, the controller directs the pilot to a runway; if the airport is busy, the plane is fitted into a traffic pattern with other aircraft waiting to land. As the plane nears the runway, the pilot is asked to contact the tower. There, another controller, who also is watching the plane on radar, monitors the aircraft the last mile or so to the runway, delaying any departures that would interfere with the plane's landing.

Once the plane has landed, a ground controller in the tower directs it along the taxiways to its assigned gate. The ground controller usually works entirely by sight, but may use radar if visibility is very poor.

The procedure is reversed for departures. The ground controller directs the plane to the proper runway. The local controller then informs the pilot about conditions at the airport, such as the weather, speed and direction of wind, and visibility. The local controller also issues runway clearance for the pilot to take off. Once in the air, the plane is guided out of the airport's airspace by the departure controller.

After each plane departs, airport tower controllers notify enroute controllers who will next take charge. There are twenty-two enroute control centers located around the country, each employing 300 to 700 controllers, with more than 150 on duty during peak hours at the busier facilities. Airplanes generally fly along designated routes; each center is assigned a certain airspace containing many different routes.

In addition to airport towers and enroute centers, air traffic controller specialists also work in flight service stations operated at over 100 locations. These specialists provide pilots with information on the station's particular area, including terrain, preflight and in-flight weather information, suggested routes, and other information important to the safety of a flight. Flight service station specialists help pilots in emergency situations and participate in searches for missing or overdue aircraft. However, they are not involved in actively managing air traffic.

TRAINING

Pilots

All pilots who are paid to transport passengers or cargo must have a commercial pilot's license with an instrument rating issued by the FAA. Helicopter pilots must hold a commercial pilot's certificate with a helicopter rating. To qualify for these licenses, applicants must be at least eighteen years old and have at least 250 hours of flight experience. The time can be reduced through participation in certain school curricula approved by the FAA.

They also must pass a strict physical examination to make sure that they are in good health and have 20/20 vision with or without glasses, good hearing, and no physical handicaps that could impair their performance. Applicants must pass a written test that includes questions on the principles of safe flight, navigation techniques, and FAA regulations. They also must demonstrate their flying ability to FAA or designated examiners.

To fly in periods of low visibility pilots must be rated by the FAA to fly by instruments. Pilots may qualify for this rating by having a total of 105 hours of flight experience, including forty hours of experience in flying by instruments; passing a written examination on procedures and FAA regulations covering instrument flying; and demonstrating their ability to fly by instruments.

Airline pilots must fulfill additional requirements. They must pass FAA written and flight examinations to earn a flight engineer's license. Captains must have an airline transport pilot's license. Applicants for this license must be at least twenty-three years old and have a minimum of 1,500 hours of flying experience, including night and instrument flying.

All licenses are valid as long as a pilot can pass the periodic physical examinations and tests of flying skills required by government and company regulations.

The armed forces have always been an important source of trained pilots for civilian jobs. Military pilots gain valuable experience on jet aircraft and helicopters, and persons with this experience are generally preferred. This primarily reflects the extensive flying time military pilots receive. The FAA has certified about 600 civilian flying schools, including some colleges and universities that offer degree credit for pilot training. In recent years, the armed services have increased financial incentives in an effort to retain more pilots. This has shifted more of the burden for training pilots to FAA certified schools. Over the next several years, the number of available pilots who have been trained in the military should increase as reductions in military budgets result in more pilots leaving military service. Over the long haul, however, fewer pilots will be trained by the armed forces and this will mean that FAA certified schools will do more of the training.

Although some small airlines will hire high school graduates, most airlines require two years of college and prefer to hire college graduates. In fact, most entrants to this occupation have a college degree. If the number of college-educated applicants increases, employers may raise their educational requirements. Because pilots must be able to make quick decisions and accurate judgments under pressure, airline companies reject applicants who do not pass required psychological and aptitude tests.

New airline pilots usually start as copilots. Although airlines favor applicants who already have a flight engineer's license, they may train those who have only the commercial license. All new pilots receive several weeks of intensive training in simulators and classrooms before being assigned to a flight.

Organizations other than airlines generally require less flying experience. However, a commercial pilot's license is a minimum requirement, and employers prefer applicants who have experience in the type of craft they will be flying. New employees usually start as copilots or flying less sophisticated equipment. Test pilots often are required to have an engineering degree.

Flight Attendants

The airlines prefer to hire people who are poised, tactful, and resourceful and who can deal comfortably with strangers. Applicants usually must be at least nineteen to twenty-one years old, but some airlines have higher minimum age requirements. Flight attendants must fall into a specific weight range depending on their height and must have excellent health, good vision, and the ability to speak clearly.

Applicants must be high school graduates. Those having several years of college or experience in dealing with the public are preferred. More and more attendants being hired are college graduates. Flight attendants for international airlines generally must speak an appropriate foreign language fluently.

Most large airlines require that newly hired flight attendants complete four to six weeks of intensive training in their own schools. The airlines that do not operate schools generally send new employees to the school of another airline. Transportation to the training centers and an allowance for board, room, and school supplies may be provided. Trainees learn emergency procedures such as evacuating an airplane, operating an oxygen system, and giving first aid. Attendants also are taught flight regulations and duties, and company operations and policies. Trainees receive instruction on personal grooming and weight control. Trainees for the international routes get additional instruction in passport and customs regulations and dealing with terrorism. Toward the end of their training, students go on practice flights. Attendants must receive twelve to fourteen hours of training in emergency procedures and passenger relations annually.

After completing the initial training, flight attendants are assigned to one of their airline's bases. New attendants are placed in reserve status and are called on either to staff extra flights or fill in for attendants who are sick or on vacation. Reserve attendants on duty must be available on short notice. Attendants usually remain on reserve for at least one year; at some cities, it may take five years or longer to advance from reserve status. Advancement takes longer today than in the past because experienced attendants are remaining in this career for more years than they used to. Attendants who no longer are on reserve bid for regular assignments. Because these assignments are based on seniority, usually only the most experienced attendants get their choice of base and flights.

Some attendants transfer to flight service instructor, customer service director, recruiting representative, or various other administrative positions.

Air Traffic Controllers

Air traffic controller trainees are selected through the competitive federal civil service system. Applicants must pass a written test that measures their ability to learn the controller's duties. Applicants with experience as a pilot, navigator, or military controller can improve their rating by scoring well on the occupational knowledge portion of the examination. Abstract reasoning and three-dimensional spatial visualization are among the aptitudes the exam measures. In addition, applicants generally must have three years of general work experience or four years of college, or a combination of both. Applicants also must survive a one-week screening at the FAAs Aeronautical Center Academy in Oklahoma City that includes aptitude tests using computer simulators, physical and psychological examinations. Successful applicants receive drug screening tests.

For airport tower and enroute center positions, applicants must be less than thirty-one years old. Those thirty-one years old and over are eligible for positions at flight-service stations.

Controllers must be articulate, because directions to pilots must be given quickly and clearly. Intelligence and a good memory also are important because controllers constantly receive information that they must immediately grasp, interpret, and remember. Decisiveness is also required because controllers often have to make quick decisions. The ability to concentrate is crucial because controllers must make these decisions in the midst of noise and other distractions.

Trainees learn their craft through a combination of formal and on-the-job training. They receive three to four months of intensive training at the FAA academy, where they learn the fundamentals of the airway system, FAA regulations, controller equipment, aircraft performance characteristics, as well as more specialized tasks. Based on aptitude and test scores, trainees are selected to work at either an enroute center or a tower. Regardless of the type of training, students must demonstrate their ability to make quick, correct decisions in simulated air traffic situations. After graduation, it takes several years of progressively more responsible work experience, interspersed with considerable classroom instruction and independent study, to become a fully qualified controller. This training includes instruction in the operation of the new, more automated air traffic control system including the automated Microwave Landing System that enables pilots to receive instructions over automated data links that is being installed in control sites across the country.

At airports, new controllers begin by supplying pilots with basic flight data and airport information. They then advance to ground controller, then local controller, departure controller, and finally, arrival controller. At an enroute traffic control center, new controllers first deliver printed flight plans to teams, gradually advancing to radar associate controller and then radar controller.

Failure to become certified in any position at a facility within a specified time may result in dismissal. Controllers who fail to complete either the academy or the on-the-job portion of the training are usually dismissed. Controllers must pass a physical examination each year and a job performance examination twice each year.

JOB OUTLOOK

Pilots

Pilots are expected to face considerable competition for jobs through 2006 because the number of applicants for new positions is expected to exceed the number of job openings. Competition will be especially keen early in the projection period due to a temporary increase in the pool of qualified pilots seeking jobs. Mergers and bankruptcies during the recent restructuring of the industry caused a large number of airline pilots to lose their jobs. Also, federal budget reductions resulted in many pilots leaving the armed forces. These and other qualified pilots seek jobs in this occupation because it offers very high earnings, glamour, prestige, and free or low cost travel benefits. As time passes, some pilots will fail to maintain their qualifications and the number of applicants competing for each opening should decline. Factors affecting demand, however, are not expected to ease that competition.

Relatively few jobs will be created from rising demand for pilots as employment is expected to increase about as fast as average for all occupations through 2006. The expected growth in airline passenger and cargo traffic will create a need for more airliners, pilots, and flight instructors. However, computerized flight management systems on new aircraft will eliminate the need for flight engineers on those planes, thus restricting the growth of pilot employment. In addition, the trend toward using larger planes in the airline industry will increase pilot productivity. Future business travel could also be adversely affected by advances in teleconferencing and facsimile mail and the elimination of many middle-management positions in corporate downsizing. Employment of business pilots is expected to grow more slowly than in the past as more businesses opt to fly with regional and smaller airlines serving their area rather than buy and operate their own aircraft. On the other hand, helicopter pilots are expected to grow more rapidly as the demand expands for the type of services helicopters can offer.

Job openings resulting from the need to replace pilots who retire or leave the occupation traditionally have been very low. Aircraft pilots understandably have an extremely strong attachment to their occupation because it requires a substantial investment in specialized training that is not transferable to other fields and it generally offers very high earnings. However, many of the pilots who were hired in the late 1960s during the last major industry boom are approaching the age for mandatory retirement, so during the projected period, retirements of pilots are expected to increase and generate several thousand job openings each year.

Pilots who have logged the greatest number of flying hours in the more sophisticated equipment generally have the best prospects. This is the reason military pilots usually have an advantage over other applicants. Job seekers with the most

FAA licenses will also have a competitive advantage. Opportunities for pilots in the regional commuter airlines and international service are expected to be more favorable as these segments are expected to grow faster than other segments of the industry.

Employment of pilots is sensitive to cyclical swings in the economy. During recessions, when a decline in the demand for air travel forces airlines to curtail the number of flights, airlines may temporarily furlough some pilots. Commercial and corporate flying, flight instruction, and testing of new aircraft also decline during recessions, adversely affecting pilots employed in those areas.

Flight Attendants

Opportunities should be favorable for people seeking flight attendant jobs as the number of applicants is expected to be roughly in balance with the number of job openings. Those with at least two years of college and experience in dealing with the public should have the best chance of being hired.

As airline restrictions on employment have been abolished, turnover—which traditionally was very high—has declined. Therefore, the majority of job openings through 2006 should be due to replacement needs. Many flight attendants are attracted to the occupation by the glamour of the airline industry and the opportunity to travel, but some eventually leave in search of jobs that offer higher earnings and require fewer nights spent away from their families. Several thousand job openings will arise each year as a result of the need to replace flight attendants who transfer to another occupation or who leave the labor force.

Employment of flight attendants is expected to grow faster than the average for all occupations through 2006. Growth in population and income is expected to increase the number of airline passengers. Airlines enlarge their capacity by increasing the number and size of planes in operation. Since Federal Aviation Administration safety rules require one attendant for every fifty seats, more flight attendants will be needed.

Employment of flight attendants is sensitive to cyclical swings in the economy. During recessions, when the demand for air travel declines, many flight attendants are put on part-time status or laid off. Until demand increases, few new flight attendants are hired.

Air Traffic Controllers

Competition for air traffic controller jobs is expected to remain extremely keen because the occupation attracts many more qualified applicants than the small number of job openings stemming from growth of the occupation and replacement needs. Turnover is very low; because of the relatively high pay and liberal retirement benefits, controllers have a very strong attachment to the occupation. Most of the current work force was hired as a result of the controller's strike during the 1980s, so the average age of current controllers is fairly young. Most controllers will not be eligible to retire until 2006 or later.

Employment of air traffic controllers is expected to show little or no change through 2006. Employment growth is not expected to keep pace with growth in the number of aircraft flying because of the implementation of a new air traffic control system over the next ten years. This computerized system will assist the controller by automatically making many of the routine decisions. Automation will allow controllers to handle more traffic, thus increasing their productivity.

Air traffic controllers who continue to meet the proficiency and medical requirements enjoy more job security than most workers. The demand for air travel and the workloads of air traffic controllers decline during recessions, but controllers seldom are laid off.

SALARIES

Pilots

Earnings of airline pilots are among the highest in the nation. According to the Future Aviation Professionals of America (FAPA), the 1996 average starting salary for airline pilots ranged from about $15,000 at the smaller turboprop airlines to $26,290 at the larger major airlines. Average earnings for experienced pilots with six years of experience ranged from $28,100 at the turboprop airlines to almost $76,800 at the largest airlines. Some senior captains on the largest aircraft earned as much as $200,000 a year. Earnings depend on factors such as the type, size, and maximum speed of the plane, and the number of hours and miles flown. Extra pay may be given for night and international flights. Generally, pilots working outside the airlines earn lower salaries. Usually, pilots who fly jet aircraft earn higher salaries than nonjet pilots.

Data from the FAPA for 1996 show that commercial helicopter pilots averaged from $33,700 to $59,900 a year. Average pay for corporate helicopter pilots ranged from $47,900 to $72,500. Some helicopter pilots earned more than $100,000 a year.

Airline pilots generally are eligible for life and health insurance plans financed by the airlines. They also receive retirement benefits, and if they fail the FAA physical examination at some point in their careers, they get disability payments. In addition, pilots receive an expense allowance, or "per diem," for every hour they are away from home. Per diem can represent up to $500 each month in addition to their salary. Some airlines also provide allowances to pilots for purchasing and cleaning their uniforms. As an additional benefit, pilots and their immediate families usually are entitled to free or reduced fare transportation on their own and other airlines.

Most airline pilots are members of unions. Most airline pilots are members of the Airline Pilots Association, International, but those employed by one major airline are members of the Allied Pilots Association. Some flight engineers are members of the Flight Engineers' International Association.

Flight Attendants

Beginning flight attendants had median earnings of about $12,800 a year in 1996, according to data from the Association of Flight Attendants. Flight attendants with six years of flying experience had median annual earnings of about $19,000, while some senior flight attendants earned as much as $40,000 a year.

Flight attendants receive extra compensation for night and international flights and for increased hours. In addition, flight attendants and their immediate families are entitled to free fares on their own airline and reduced fares on most other airlines.

Many flight attendants belong to the Association of Flight Attendants. Others may be members of the Transport Workers Union of America, the International Brotherhood of Teamsters, or other unions.

Flight attendants are required to buy uniforms and wear them while on duty. Uniform replacement items are usually paid for by the company. The airlines generally provide a small allowance to cover cleaning and upkeep of the uniforms.

Air Traffic Controllers

Air traffic controllers who started with the FAA in 1997 earned about $29,500 a year. Controllers at higher federal pay grade levels earned 5 percent more than other federal workers in an equivalent grade. A controller's pay is determined by both the worker's job responsibilities and the complexity of the particular facility. Earnings are higher at facilities where traffic patterns are more complex. In 1997, controllers averaged about $46,000 a year.

In 1997, the FAA began to implement a new, more flexible pay classification. The system features twelve grade levels instead of five and pay is based upon how many aircraft a controller works. The program provides a 10 percent overall increase in base pay for about 2,200 personnel at seven of the FAA's busiest air traffic control facilities.

Depending on length of service, air traffic controllers receive thirteen to twenty-six days of paid vacation and thirteen days of paid sick leave each year, life insurance, and health benefits. In addition, controllers can retire at an earlier age and with fewer years of service than other federal employees. Air traffic controllers are eligible to retire at age fifty with twenty years of service as an active air traffic controller or after twenty-five years of active service at any age. There is a mandatory retirement age of fifty-six for controllers who manage air traffic.

RELATED FIELDS

Pilots

Although they are not in the cockpit, air traffic controllers and dispatchers also play an important role in making sure flights are safe and on schedule, and participate in many of the decisions pilots must make.

Flight Attendants

Other jobs that involve helping people as a safety professional and require the ability to be pleasant even under trying circumstances include emergency medical technician, firefighter, and maritime crew.

Air Traffic Controllers

Other occupations that involve the direction and control of traffic in air transportation are airline-radio operator and airplane dispatcher.

INTERVIEW
Rudy Vanderkrogt
Pilot

Rudy Vanderkrogt has been in commercial aviation since 1978, when he started as a bush pilot in northern Canada. He now is a pilot with Cathay Pacific Airways in Hong Kong.

How Rudy Vanderkrogt Got Started

"As a child I always had a fascination with aircraft, airliners, in particular. This stayed with me until my high school days, when I decided to do something about it at the age of sixteen, the minimum age to hold a private pilot's license. During my teenage years I had all sorts of small jobs, shoveling snow, mowing lawns, a paper route. The money I earned I saved for my training.

"The first idea I had was to look for training through the Air Cadets and the Air Force. However, I had a disability; I wore eyeglasses. During high school the school held an annual career day. There I was also told by the chief pilot of an international airline in Canada that I would not be able to qualify as an airline pilot because of my vision. In an effort to find something in the same field, I ended up in the control tower at my local airport and was told that I could enhance my chances if I held a private pilot's license (PPL). So, I went down to the local flying school and, for what was lot of money, did my training for my PPL. I did this during my summer holidays.

"During my last year in high school I pooled the cost with other students and we rented a Cessna 172 so I could build up my hours. I needed enough hours to begin training for my commercial pilot's license (CPL). I did this at the same flying school. It also included a night flying rating and a float plane rating. By the time I was nineteen, I had the minimum requirements for getting a commercial flying job.

"My first flying job in those days was in the Canadian bush. I went out on the road in Ontario, Canada, and began knocking on doors. I was lucky. At the third place I ran into a gentleman who was looking for a pilot to fly a C-180 on floats. I had done a C-180 rating a few days before just to help me out and it paid off.

"This job turned out to be for an Indian Co-op; the reservation was located north of any developed towns, and they needed someone to get supplies and people into their community. I lived in a log cabin that was about twenty by twenty feet, no electricity, and water came from the lake fifteen feet from the front door. It wasn't what I ever planned on when I was young, but I did it gladly because it kept me in the air, and for a change I was being paid for it. It was a means to an end—build up your hours and get a better job.

"A great number of years went by from that first job. From company to company, each move brought me a better aircraft rating and more experience. I lived and worked in the Arctic, Manitoba, and British Columbia, and still could not get a job with an airline.

"I had decided sometime before that if I did not get into an airline by the time I was twenty-seven, I would go overseas and try my luck there. So I went to Australia, flew a float plane for a pearling company, and then finally got a job on a turbine pow-ered Fokker-27. Once I got this endorsement on the F-27, I was finally getting closer to what an airline wanted, and ten years after my first job I got a job on a Boeing 737 for a company that was based in Micronesia. This company paid for my training, but shortly afterward the job ended because of an industrial dis-pute. I fortunately found another job in the South Pacific, again on B737s. More experience and I was on my way to the Mid-dle East, where an even larger airline offered me work on the B737, and soon afterward put me on the new B767-300. This now had me flying long haul international flights from London to Sydney, Australia, and a hundred places in between. To me it was all that I had ever wanted, and more. I spent three and a half years doing this and then my present company, Cathay Pacific, offered me employment flying the B747-400. This was the final move; a B747-400 is the top of the ladder for an airline pilot, and after thirteen years of chasing jobs around the world I finally got to the top."

What the Job's Really Like

"When you begin with most airlines, you follow a seniority sys-tem, and that means starting over again at the bottom of the list when you change jobs. So, the first job will usually be as a first officer or copilot. This job is in name only because, in reality, you have the same qualifications as the captain. But the airline needs only so many captains and you have to do your time in the right seat before you get promoted to the left—which is where the captain sits. He also gets more money and is respon-sible for the aircraft and crew. As a first officer, you generally fly the airplane half of the time, and do paperwork and radio communications the other half.

"The best way I can describe the job is to say it's hours of boredom interspersed with moments of sheer terror. It is, how-ever, for most pilots the place to be. It beats any office job. It changes on every flight—the weather, passengers, unexpected delays, the list goes on and on. In most cases the pressure does build up and in some cases makes the job more difficult than most. Not only do you have to think about yourself, there can be as many as 400 passengers behind you.

"An average day for me on the long haul flights starts late in the evening. After a day of trying to rest, I leave home at about 9:00 P.M. The trip to the airport takes one and a half hours. When I get to work, I spend about ninety minutes reading company memos and going through flight planning. This involves checking weather at our destination and at an airport that we will go to if, for some reason, we can't land at our destination. We then look at things such as fuel, takeoff times, and who will do the takeoff and landing.

"By the time we get to the aircraft it is about one hour before takeoff. We program the computers, check and set up the aircraft systems, and make sure the fuel and cargo are all loaded on properly.

"Once all of that has been completed, we begin the procedure of getting air traffic control clearances, starting engines, doing system checks, and taxiing out for takeoff.

"The first half hour of flight is very busy. Once we are at cruising level and autopilot is in control and everything is normal, we just sit there, monitoring all systems and fuel to make sure things are going as planned.

"About two hours before we land things begin to happen again. We do checks of weather, fuel, and which runway we will be using. We then program all this information into the computer and begin our descent.

"The last half hour to forty minutes carries a heavy workload, ending with the landing and the taxi into the parking bay. The final part of the flight is again paperwork and the trip to the hotel, where we will spend about thirty hours before we return to the airport and do it all again.

"On an average month we spend about eighty-five hours in the pilot's seat. It might sound like a good deal, but often the time spent on the ground doing flight planning and cockpit preparation is never acknowledged.

"The people we work with are all dedicated professionals who love their jobs. There is a high level of camaraderie and we all try to make the most out of each trip. People we work with have a wide range of interests, and come from many backgrounds. We are in a position to learn a lot from each other.

"A downside of the job is that it is an industry in which pilots are often attacked as overpaid and underworked. The jet lag is also a downside. It's difficult to adjust to and it's cumulative. You don't really get over it until you have a long leave.

"But I am doing a job I love. I like the variety of destinations, the crew, the passengers, and the working hours. I have lots of days off at home with my family.

"The salary and benefits are good, too. I earn about $12,000 a month, plus housing, travel, and schooling allowances.

"These extra allowances are given because I work as an expatriate; I am not a local hire. The cost of housing in Hong Kong is among the highest in the world. Our modest flat costs $5,500 month. This airline and most others also pay per diems in local currency at the destination to cover your meals.

"Salary is based on job title and years of service. Many other airlines structure their salaries on job title, years of service, and the type and size of aircraft.

"If you get your first job with an airline in the United States, you would expect to earn around $2,000 a month. If your first job is in general aviation, you would expect to earn less."

Expert Advice

"You have to have a love of aviation. You have to be sure of what you want and be determined to follow through. You don't suddenly become an airline pilot. You start at the bottom where the pay and conditions are less than you would have hoped for.

"Pilots are technical, logical, and analytical people. You may be called upon to sum up the situation and make a decision in a short period of time that will affect your life and the lives of your passengers.

"To get started you can go the way of a military career or go to your local flying school or buy an aviation magazine and apply to a flying academy advertised there.

"In summary, if you have thought of a career in aviation, there is so much more than the Air Force or airlines. If you really enjoy this sort of work, get in and do it. Yes, there will be obstacles, but pilots are people who will overcome these and get on with the job."

INTERVIEW
Jim Carr
Pilot

Jim Carr has been flying since 1967. He is a Boeing 757 captain with America West. He got his commercial license when he was in the air force and has been flying commercially since 1980.

In 1971 he earned his B.S. in Aerospace Engineering and Mechanics from the University of Minnesota in Minneapolis.

How Jim Carr Got Started

"As far back as I can remember I was fascinated with airplanes. As a little kid I had a strong interest in them. While I was on a summer job between high school and college, a friend brought in a $5 coupon for an introductory offer to fly your first lesson. It was just awesome. That gave me the bug and I continued after that and got my private license. I flew a little bit through college and once I graduated from college I went into the air force and stayed there for ten years.

"I first started flying for Air Florida. That was in 1980. After two years I moved to Phoenix where I am now, with America West.

"I started out as a line pilot and was asked to join the management group in 1985. I became the assistant chief pilot and ultimately the chief pilot. Then in 1987 I became Vice President of Flight Operations. I stayed with that position until February of 1995. All through my administrative tenure I continued to fly. Now I fly full-time."

What the Job's Really Like

"Typical to a day's work is checking in about an hour prior to departure time. We go to our dispatch center, which has a lot of computers and individuals who plan all the flights, monitor the weather, and so forth. They provide us with a flight plan—the route of flight that we have filed with the air traffic controllers. We sign off on that, then from that point we proceed to the airplane and we do a series of preflight checks. These include verifying the maintenance data, a preflight inspection of both the exterior of the plane—we're looking for any apparent damage or anything that looks abnormal, leaks, that sort of thing—then a cockpit check before we leave the gate.

"Most modern turbojet airliners now have two pilots, a captain and a first officer. We do our checks, then ultimately we go over a formal checklist to ensure that all the switches and controls are in the proper position before we leave the gate.

"There's activity galore during that process. The fuelers are fueling the plane, the flight attendants are doing their own safety checks, then we start boarding passengers. There's just a lot of activity as we get closer and closer to the push back time, our published departure time. The push back is when we back off from the gate.

"We taxi out to an assigned runway and are cleared for takeoff and away we go. It's a matter of flying the airplane and accomplishing the procedures set by the FAA. Ninety-nine point nine percent of the flights are routine. When something happens, we analyze the situation and take whatever appropriate action is necessary. I've never had what I'd call a close call. I've had hydraulic systems fail and an engine quit, but we're trained to handle that. An airplane can fly quite well with only one engine operating. It's really a testament to the equipment we're flying these days. There are so many backup systems, rarely do you ever have a serious problem.

"On top of that every six months we're back in the simulator practicing. In a two-hour simulator session a pilot can experience more emergencies than he or she would ever experience in a career.

"Landing is one of the most fun parts. I think most pilots enjoy that the most. You're actually manipulating the aircraft controls with your hands and feet, as opposed to letting the autopilot fly. Flying is really just a series of correcting for the last mistake that was made. That's not a negative statement. Flying an aircraft in our atmosphere is just a real dynamic situation and so you're constantly making corrections to get the airplane from point A to point B.

"Once we land the work isn't over. We have to find our way to the gate. Sometimes that can be more difficult than finding the airport from the air. There are many more dangers on the ground than there are in the air. There are many vehicles and people—you have to keep your eyes peeled.

"We have a shutdown checklist, then we fill out the maintenance log, then I'm cleared to leave. If I'm back at my domicile, I head home. If I'm on the road, we gather up the crew and go out to the curb and take a shuttle to the hotel where we spend our layover. The layover can be anywhere from nine to twenty-four hours. The purpose of the layover is to rest up for your next flight.

"The downside is that you have to spend extended periods away from your family. Most airline pilots will fly anywhere from sixty to eighty-five hours a month, which doesn't sound like a lot if you compare it with a forty- or fifty-hour work week, but to get that amount of flight time, you're on duty for upwards of 300 hours a month.

"A lot of people who don't do much traveling really like to stay in a hotel once in a while, it's a nice change of pace, for example, you don't have to make your bed yourself. However, most hotels start looking pretty much the same after awhile. It seems that you spend an awful lot of time in hotels, just waiting for the airplane to come back so you can leave. You can use that time to read and do other things, but it still seems like endless periods of time.

"And during a long flight, you have to fight boredom and fatigue. You take a break, get up, walk around, and talk with your copilot.

"My routes vary from month to month. That's typical of most airlines. The pilots are given flight schedules based on their seniority and their choice of published schedules for the coming month. My schedule over the last few months has been flying from Phoenix to Chicago and Phoenix to Newark, New Jersey, or New York City.

"It's not so much the preference of the airport or the route, it provides the specific days off I need for personal business. Unlike a professional who works in an office, if I need to take the car in I can't just say I'll be in late. When I have a flight leaving I can't take the car in. You have to plan those types of things a little bit further in advance. Usually I fly three or four days a week. Typically, it will be a three-day trip. You leave home, you're gone for two nights, and you're back on the third. You might come in and fly another one- or two-day trip during the week. But I can choose my days off more or less. And the time off away from duty is yours.

"I love the flying part most of all—to be up in the sky and to be able to look at the wonders of nature. You get to see thunderstorms, weather fronts, and wind storms up close. It's certainly a view of the world not everyone gets to see, at least not with the frequency we do.

"The upsides are the potential for a very nice income. Most starting salaries are about $30,000, then it goes up to $45,000 to $50,000 by the second year. The big jump is when you become a captain and move over to the left seat. Twelve years into the company, captains at America West are making about $115,000 a year. At other airlines, flying similar aircraft, pilots are making $150,000 to $180,000.

"Generally, we work under the seniority system. All promotions and upward movement depend upon when you were hired. So, if you were to switch airlines, you'd be starting from the bottom again.

"I'm kind of biased, but I think it's the greatest job in the free world. Most pilots feel real fortunate that we do a job we really enjoy doing. And while I look forward to having time off, at the end of my three or four days off I'm always looking forward to going back to work. Not many people in the workforce have that same feeling."

Expert Advice

"I would advise you to work real hard in school and get as good a background in mathematics and science as you possibly can. The more modern the aircraft cockpits and systems become, the more that type of a science/engineering/mathematics background really helps to understand how all of it works. We don't have to build the airplanes, but situations come up that a deeper understanding really helps in troubleshooting problems.

"Another thing is that you have to be really conscious of your health and adopt a healthy lifestyle."

INTERVIEW
Gracie Anderson
Flight Attendant

Gracie Anderson started with America West after a three-month train-
ing program. She has been a flight attendant for more than a dozen
years.

How Gracie Anderson Got Started

"I did this on a bet. Back in 1985 my brother-in-law told me that America West was hiring, so I called them up. They put me through three or four interviews and that's how I ended up getting the job. The first interview was a group interview with about thirty other applicants. You had to get up and talk about yourself and say what you were doing at that time. Then it went to a smaller group interview and they gave you little assignments to do. What if such and such happened, what would you do? That sort of thing. Then it went to a one-on-one interview.

"I got the job. At America West at the time, we were what they called 'cross-utilized.' That meant that not only were we flight attendants, we also worked reservations, the ticket counter at the gate, and down at the ramp. You were never just flying. Three days a week I'd fly, the other days I'd be at the gate or whatever.

"I also went into the training department for a while and taught reservation clerks. I fly full-time now. Cross-utilizations became defunct in 1989 or 1990. But every once in a while I still go off the line and do in-flight training for attendants."

What the Job's Really Like

"The work is exhausting—you're on your feet a lot, you have very strange hours. And the time differences really affect you. I fly to Chicago and Newark and my overnights are in San

Diego. But I have a lot of other choices, too. We fly coast to coast and all points in between.

"We look at ourselves as the most important safety feature on the aircraft. That's because of our knowledge of how to get out and what to do. But a lot of the passengers are only thinking about getting their Cokes. If they don't get it as soon as they want it, they think their lives are over. They don't look at us as the people who will save them if anything should happen.

"Our primary role is safety; secondary is service. But being in the transportation business, you really have to play up the service part of it.

"During takeoff we're very busy. Probably the most exhausting part of the flight is just getting everybody on. I try to remember that, when I have 100 plus people on my flight, they're not all on vacation. Some are going for work, some have just lost somebody near to them. Or they just lost the biggest deal of their lives or they're going to present the biggest deal of their lives. And they're all sitting in this tiny little tube together and the emotions are just running the gamut.

"Add the fear of flying to that—well, it's not routine for them; there is stress and a lot of nerves.

"Dealing with the passengers can be the hardest part. Recently, on a flight, even before we left, I had a passenger who was back in the bathroom smoking. One of the other flight attendants said something to her about it, but she denied it. Later on, we were really delayed, and as we got closer to Phoenix she came back to ask for something to drink and I could smell the cigarette smoke. I understand the addiction because I used to smoke, but it's not so much that she snuck a cigarette, it's the fact that she lied to me and I don't know where she put her cigarette. That's where our biggest fear comes from, causing a fire. I put on gloves and went through the trash can in the rest room. This is where the glamour comes in. It was really disgusting. I found the butt in the trash can along with nothing but paper.

"We also have to serve the food. We turn the ovens on and heat up the food, then place the trays in the cart to pass out. But passengers can get so impatient. It's not as if we can stand up right after takeoff. We have headsets to pass out, too, if there's a movie, and someone else is passing out the drinks. And in the middle of all of this, there's always a passenger asking,

'Can I have a pillow? Can I change seats? What about my connection?' It's constant questions. And that's why sometimes passing out the food or drinks takes longer. We're constantly getting interrupted. But, then that's what we're there for.

"It's easy to feel harried. It's not like you're out of control or anything, but sometimes you wish they'd just give you five minutes.

"And it's easy to feel unappreciated. I've been talked to horribly. But the majority of people I deal with are really very nice. But you always have that handful. And you have to realize they're like that to everyone. You just have to keep your sense of humor. And it always feels really good to get home.

"At the beginning the travel part was great, I was single and you'd go out and have fun in different cities. But as time wore on that kind of got old. Now I'm married and I have twin daughters. Sometimes my husband comes with me on my overnight flights, and that's fun. But my objective is different now. Get there, do my trip, and come home.

"The time off is unbelievable. I can't beat it. It's about nineteen days off a month. I get to see my kids more than most people. I've gotten to see more of the world than I ever thought I would. Although we don't anymore, America West used to fly overseas. I've flown to Nagoya, Japan, for example. I might not have picked it as a vacation spot, but still I got to see it, had my hotel paid for—it was great. I've been to Hawaii, too, I don't know how many times, then just around the states. It's been unbelievable. Plus, you get more or less free flights when you're not working. You also get car rental and hotel discounts.

"Salaries are another downside though. It's not like what it used to be. The older attendants make anywhere from $40,000 to $60,000. But the airline started what they call a 'B' scale for the new hirees. They start off somewhere around $12,000 or $13,000 a year.

"Sometimes I sit there and I think, what are we doing? We're a flying restaurant sailing through the sky with a hundred thousand pounds of fuel under us. Who in their right mind is going to get into this thing?

"But most of the people are really, really wonderful. You'll have someone come up to you and say that it's been the best flight they ever had and that makes up for everything."

Expert Advice

"I think if you're young and have a lot of energy, it's wonderful. I always joke around and say I'm donning my rhino skin. You need thick skin to do this. I have a flight buddy who teases me and says I'm like Mary Poppins out there. That's what I'm here for. I'm not here to make these people have a miserable trip. I have a hard time saying 'no' to them. It has to be something outlandish. I try not to get bothered by petty things. You're going to see a lot of pettiness, but you can't let it get to you. I had a gentleman who had won a lot of stuffed animals. They were all packed away in the overhead bin. Then another passenger comes in and opens up the bin. All of a sudden he starts throwing all these animals. I looked over and I saw a giraffe flying through the cabin, then an elephant, and a monkey. He thinks it's his bin because it's over his seat. So, sometimes you have to go up to them and say, 'No, it's my bin and I'm sharing it with everyone.' Sometimes you have to treat them as if they're first-graders. I know it sounds silly, but I try to give people little Life Lessons. If someone doesn't say please to me, if they say, 'Hey, gimme a Coke,' I smile and say, 'What's the magic word?' I do it with a smile. I've been able to say things to people and get away with it, but you have to be able to wear that smile.

"The key to success in this industry is that you have to be extremely flexible. Different things happen all the time—you get canceled, delayed, and diverted. You have to be able to go with the flow.

"And you can't be chasing the almighty dollar to work at this job. You have to want just time off and flight benefits. That's really where the fun is. I love it. Where else could you put in so little time and have such good benefits?"

INTERVIEW
Karen Seals
Air Traffic Controller

As an air traffic controller, Karen Seals is employed by the Federal Aviation Administration. She is assigned to Phoenix Airport, but is currently on temporary assignment at Goodyear, a small airport just to the west of Phoenix.

How Karen Seals Got Started

"I have always loved flying and airplanes. My father is a pilot and we were able to fly quite a bit as kids and that's where my initial exposure came from.

"I was previously employed as a geologist in the '80s, but it was in one of the down cycles and continued to stay in a down cycle. I kept getting laid off and needed to find a different job. So, since I'd always had a love for aviation, I decided it was time to get out of geology and get some different training so I could work at something more stable.

"I studied at the University of Colorado in Boulder and graduated in 1984 with a B.A. in geology. In 1986 I just opened the phone book and started making calls to the different airports until I finally got the right number for a regional office of the FAA. I asked them how I could become an air traffic controller and they told me that I needed to sign up to take a test. It was an aptitude test with different portions to it. You had to have a fairly high score. I took the test, then ended up waiting a year and a half before they called me. There was a backlog then. While I was waiting, I didn't really think I would hear from them. There had been no contact at all in that year and a half. Then I got a phone call out of the blue. They said they had a date available at the academy in Oklahoma City. It happened to be coming up in the next week. I packed up and went out there. The course took four months.

"During the training I stayed in an apartment set up specifically to accommodate the FAA. We were paid a salary and a per diem during the training period.

"After I graduated, I started off at Deer Valley Airport on the north side of Phoenix. Then I moved to Phoenix Airport."

What the Job's Really Like

"I'm responsible for the safety and the efficient flow of traffic. I sequence the airplanes into the airport for landings and for takeoffs.

"We work eight hours at a time, five days a week, but we do shift work. At Phoenix we're open seven days a week, twenty-four hours a day. At Goodyear we're open from six in the morning until nine at night. It depends on the airport. Hours can vary from week to week.

"There is stress involved with this job, but I think the stress varies from person to person. And sometimes people don't even realize what it is that causes the stress. It could be the rotating shifts, with night shifts and coming back early the next morning. That's hard to do. The interruption in your sleeping pattern can cause stress. The actual amount of air traffic can also cause stress.

"For me the most stress comes in when you really have to work together as a team. You have to interact so much, you don't work independently at all—it's all team work. And sometimes when you work with other people there can be conflicts. It's not conflicts of personality, it's just because communicating can be difficult. At a bigger airport you could have from nine to twelve controllers working together. At a small airport you work more independently; most of the time there are two on duty together.

"You only have one air space and you have to split it in half and you constantly have to do something in another controller's air space. In order to do something in that air space you have to get his or her permission. So you are constantly having to communicate and plan ahead.

"We get enough breaks during the day so that you don't get that worn out. You might work for an hour, have a break, then go back to work at a different position where you're doing something entirely different. You divide your time between ground control, where you're taxiing planes to and from the runway and local control, where you clear them for takeoff and landings. And there are several other positions, too. You get a lot of variety so you don't get tired.

"On the plus side, we get great benefits, and time off. We also get to take familiarization trips. They're for training purposes, but you can go on any airline that participates in the program and ride up in the cockpit. And you can go to whatever destination you choose. They have you do this so you can ask questions and learn what it's like in the cockpit. And you do a little liaison work, too.

"It's an exciting job. I'm always happy to go to work. I love what I do, I love to work the airplanes. You put a plan together and ask everybody to do certain things. And everybody actually does what you asked and it works out great. You're getting the airplanes out on time and you're getting them in without problems.

"Because of the way Phoenix is set up—we only have two runways—it's exciting because you're constantly having to plan. If Plan A doesn't work out, you have to have a Plan B. We run a lot of traffic on two runways. We're always busy, always pumped up. There's always something going on. We deal with more than 100 to 120 takeoffs and landings an hour.

"You also get to work in the aviation community, which is a really neat group of people. You get to see all the aspects. You get to work with the pilots, the people down on the ramp, the airport people, and the administrative people. It's such a variety of people and everyone has to depend on each other and help each other out. It's a unique experience."

Expert Advice

"Hang in there for a couple of years until the hiring starts back up. And if I were just getting out of high school and wanted to pursue this field, I would pick a school where you could get some kind of aviation training, specifically in air traffic. It's more competitive now and, though a college degree isn't necessary, the more training you have the better your chances will be."

FOR MORE INFORMATION

Pilots

Information about job opportunities in a particular airline and the qualifications required may be obtained by writing to the personnel manager of the airline. For addresses of airline companies and information about job opportunities and salaries, contact:

> Future Aviation Professionals of America
> 4291 J. Memorial Drive
> Atlanta, GA 30032

For information on airline pilots, contact:

> Airline Pilots Association
> 1625 Massachusetts Avenue NW
> Washington, DC 20036

> Air Transport Association of America
> 1709 New York Avenue NW
> Washington, DC 20006

For information on helicopter pilots, contact:

> Helicopter Association International
> 1619 Duke Street
> Alexandria, VA 22314

For a copy of List of Certificated Pilot Schools, write to:

> Superintendent of Documents
> U.S. Government Printing Office
> Washington, DC 20402

For information about job opportunities in companies other than airlines, consult the classified section of aviation trade magazines and apply to companies that operate aircraft at local airports.

Flight Attendants

Information about job opportunities in a particular airline and the qualifications required may be obtained by writing to the personnel manager of the company. For addresses of airline companies and information about job opportunities and salaries, contact:

Future Aviation Professionals of America
4959 Massachusetts Boulevard
Atlanta, GA 30337

Air Traffic Controllers

A pamphlet providing general information about controllers and instructions for submitting an application is available from any U.S. Office of Personnel Management Job Information Center. Look under U.S. Government, Office of Personnel Management, in your telephone book to obtain a local Job Information Center telephone number, and call for a copy of the Air Traffic Controller Announcement. If there is no listing in your telephone book, dial the toll-free directory assistance number at (800) 555-1212 and request the number of the Office of Personnel Management Job Information Center for your location.

CHAPTER 7 Rail Transportation Workers

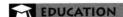
EDUCATION
H.S. preferred

$$$ SALARY/EARNINGS
$25,000 to $55,000

OVERVIEW

Rail transportation workers operate our nation's trains, subways, and streetcars to facilitate the movement of passengers and cargo. Railroad transportation workers deliver travelers and freight to destinations throughout the nation, while operators of subways and streetcars provide passenger service within a single metropolitan area.

Railroad Transportation Workers

Locomotive engineers and rail yard engineers are among the most highly skilled workers on the railroad. They operate locomotives in yards, stations, and over the tracks between distant stations and yards. Locomotive engineers operate trains carrying cargo and passengers between stations, while rail yard engineers move cars within yards to assemble or disassemble trains. In addition to those engineers who work for railroads, some engineers called dinkey operators work at industrial plants or mines operating smaller engines that pull cars loaded with coal, rock, or supplies around the site.

Engineers operate the throttle to start and accelerate the train and use air brakes or dynamic brakes to slow and stop it.

They monitor gauges and meters that measure speed, fuel, temperature, battery charge, and air pressure in the brake lines. Both on the road and in the yard, they watch for signals that indicate track obstructions, other train movements, and speed limits. They must have a thorough knowledge of the signal systems, yards, and terminals along their routes and be constantly aware of the condition and makeup of their train. This is extremely important because trains react differently to acceleration, braking, and curves, depending on the number of cars, the ratio of empty to loaded cars, and the amount of slack in the train.

Most engineers run diesel locomotives; a few run electric locomotives. Before and after each run, engineers check locomotives for mechanical problems. Minor adjustments are made on the spot, but major problems are reported to the engine shop supervisor. In an effort to reduce costs, most railroads are phasing out assistant engineers, also known as firers, who monitor locomotive instruments and signals and observe the track for obstructions. Most of these duties are now performed by brake operators.

Road conductors and yard conductors are in charge of the train and yard crews. Conductors assigned to freight trains record each car's contents and destination and make sure that cars are added and removed at the proper points along the route. Conductors assigned to passenger trains collect tickets and fares and assist passengers. At stops, they signal engineers when to pull out of the station.

Before a train leaves the terminal, the road conductor and engineer discuss instructions received from the dispatcher concerning the train's route, timetable, and cargo. While underway, conductors receive additional information by radio. This may include information about track conditions ahead or instructions to pull off at the next available stop to let another train pass. During the run, conductors use two-way radios to contact engineers. They pass on instructions received from dispatchers and remind engineers of stops, reported track conditions, and the presence of other trains.

While underway, conductors receive information from brake operators regarding any equipment problems, and they may arrange for defective cars to be removed from the train for repairs at the nearest station or stop. They inform dispatchers of any problems using a radio or wayside telephone.

Yard conductors supervise the crews that assemble and disassemble trains. Some cars are sent to special tracks for unloading, while the rest are moved to other tracks to await assemblage into trains destined for different cities. Conductors tell engineers where to move cars. They tell brake operators which cars to couple and uncouple and which switches to throw to divert the locomotive or cars to the proper track. In yards that have automatic classification systems, conductors use electrical remote controls to operate the track switches that route cars to the correct track.

Brake operators play a pivotal role in making locomotives and cars into trains. Working under the direction of conductors, they do the physical work involved in adding and removing cars at railroad stations and assembling and disassembling trains in railroad yards.

Freight train crews include either one or two brake operators—one in the locomotive with the engineer and another in the rear car. An increasing number of freight trains use only one brake operator because new visual instrumentation and monitoring devices have eliminated the need for operators outside the locomotive. Before departure, brake operators inspect the train to make sure that all couplers and airhoses are fastened, that handbrakes on all the cars are released, and that the air brakes are functioning properly. While underway, they regularly look for smoke, sparks, and other signs of sticking brakes, overheated axle bearings, and other potentially faulty equipment. They may make minor repairs to airhoses and couplers. In case of unexpected stops, brake operators set up signals to protect both ends of the train.

When freight trains approach an industrial site, the brake operator in the locomotive gets off the train and runs ahead to switch the train to the proper track. They uncouple the cars and throw track switches to route them to certain tracks if they are to be unloaded, or to an outgoing train if their final destination is farther down the line. They also set hand brakes to secure cars.

Many smaller railroads operate with only two crew members—an engineer and a conductor. Most passenger trains no longer employ brake operators but employ assistant conductors to help conductors collect tickets and assist passengers.

Because trains operate twenty-four hours a day, seven days a week, many rail transportation employees often work nights, weekends, and holidays. On some days subway operators may work multiple shifts. Undesirable shifts are assigned to persons who have the least seniority.

Most freight trains are unscheduled, and, as a result, few workers on these trains have scheduled assignments. Instead, their names are placed on a list, and when their turn comes they are assigned to the next train, usually on short notice and often at odd hours. Because road service personnel often work on trains that operate between stations that are hundreds of miles apart, they may spend several nights a week away from home.

Freight and yard conductors and brake operators spend most of their time outdoors in all kinds of weather. The work of brake operators on local runs—where trains frequently stop at stations to pick up and deliver cars—is physically demanding. Climbing up and down and getting off moving cars is strenuous and can be dangerous.

Subway and Streetcar Operators

Subway operators control trains that transport passengers throughout a city and its suburbs. The trains usually run on tracks in underground tunnels, but some systems have lines that run in part on tracks on the surface or elevated above streets. Observing the system's signals, operators start, slow, or stop the subway train. They make announcements to riders, open and close the doors, and ensure that passengers get on and off the subway safely.

Operators should have a basic understanding of the operating system and be able to recognize common equipment problems. When breakdowns or emergencies occur, operators contact their dispatcher or supervisor and may have to evacuate cars. To meet predetermined schedules, operators must control the amount of time spent at each station.

Streetcar operators drive electric-powered streetcars or trolleys that transport passengers. Streetcars run on tracks that may be recessed in city streets, so operators must observe traffic signals and cope with car and truck traffic. Operators start, slow, and stop their cars so passengers may board or alight. They collect fares, and issue change and transfers. They also answer questions from passengers concerning fares, schedules, and routes.

TRAINING

Most railroad transportation workers begin as trainees for either engineer or brake operator jobs. Railroads prefer that applicants have a high school education. Applicants must have good hearing, eyesight, and color vision, as well as good hand-eye coordination, manual dexterity, and mechanical aptitude. Physical stamina is required for brake operator jobs. Most employers require that applicants for railroad transportation jobs pass a physical examination and tests that screen for drug and alcohol use.

Railroads prefer that applicants for locomotive engineer jobs be at least twenty-one years old. Engineer jobs are frequently filled by workers with experience in other railroad operating occupations, such as brake operators or conductors. Most beginning engineers undergo a six-month training program, which includes classroom and hands-on instruction in locomotive operation. At the end of the training period, aspiring engineers must pass qualifying tests covering locomotive equipment, air brake systems, fuel economy, train handling techniques, and operating rules and regulations.

On most railroads, brake operators begin by making several trips with conductors and experienced operators to become familiar with the job. On some railroads, however, new brake operators undergo extensive training, including instruction in signaling, coupling and uncoupling cars, throwing switches, and boarding moving trains.

As railroads need new engineers and brake operators, the newly trained workers who have the most seniority are placed on the "extra board." Extra board engineers and brake operators work only when the railroad needs substitutes for regular workers who are absent because of vacation, illness, or other personal reasons. Extra board engineers and brake operators frequently must wait years until they accumulate enough seniority to get a regular assignment. Seniority rules also may allow workers with seniority to select their type of assignment. For example, an engineer may move from an initial regular assignment in yard service to road service.

Engineers undergo periodic physical examinations and drug and alcohol testing to determine their fitness to operate locomotives. Unannounced safety and efficiency tests are also given to judge their overall conduct of operations. In some cases, engineers who fail to meet these physicals and pass these tests are restricted to yard service, or, in other instances, they may be disciplined, trained to perform other work, or discharged.

Conductor jobs generally are filled from the ranks of experienced brake operators who have passed tests covering signals, timetables, operating rules, and related subjects. Some companies require these tests be passed within the first few years of employment. Until permanent positions become available, new conductors are put on the extra board, where they substitute for experienced conductors who are absent. On most railroads, conductors on extra board may work as brake operators if there are not enough conductor runs available that month. Seniority usually is the main factor in determining promotion from brake operator to conductor and from extra board to a permanent position. Advancement to conductor jobs is limited because there are many more brake operators than conductors.

Most railroads maintain separate seniority lists for road service and yard service conductors. Conductors usually remain in one type of service for their entire career. On some railroads, however, conductors start in the yards, then move to freight service, and finally to passenger service. Some conductors advance to managerial or administrative positions.

For subway and streetcar operator jobs, subway transit systems prefer applicants to have a high school education. Some systems require subway operators to work as bus drivers for a specified period of time. Applicants must be in good health, articulate, and able to make quick, responsible judgments.

New operators generally are placed in training programs that last from a few weeks to six months. At the end of the period of classroom and on-the-job training, operators usually must pass qualifying examinations covering the operating system, troubleshooting, and evacuation and emergency procedures. Some operators with sufficient seniority can advance to station managers.

JOB OUTLOOK

Rail transportation workers held 83,000 jobs in 1996—including 25,000 conductors; 21,000 locomotive engineers; 18,000 brake, signal, and switch operators; and 5,000 rail yard engineers and dinkey operators. Subway and streetcar operators accounted for nearly 13,000 jobs. Railroads employ about 82 percent of all rail transportation workers. The rest work for state and local governments as subway and streetcar operators, and for mining and manufacturing establishments operating their own locomotives and rail cars to move ore, coal, and other bulk materials.

Competition for available opportunities is expected to be keen. Many people qualify for rail transportation occupations because education beyond high school is generally not required. Many more desire employment than can be hired because the pay is good and the work steady.

Employment for a majority of railroad transportation workers is expected to decline through 2006, with only locomotive engineers and subway and streetcar operators expected to grow. The total number of new jobs, however, will not be large. Also, relatively few opportunities resulting from replacement needs will occur because the attractive pay, tenure, and job security results in relatively few rail transportation workers leaving their jobs. In addition, the industry continues to reduce the workforce by eliminating positions left vacant by employees who retire from the rail industry or leave for other reasons. Mergers and divestiture-related cutbacks are also responsible for the reduction of rail occupation employment.

Demand for railroad freight service will grow as the economy and the intermodal transportation of goods expand and railroads become more efficient. Intermodal systems use trucks to pick up and deliver the shippers' sealed trailers or containers, and trains to transport them long distance. This saves customers time and money by efficiently carrying goods across country. Intermodalism is the fastest growing type of railroad transportation. For railroads, the benefit has been the increased efficiency of equipment use, allowing increases in the number of runs each train makes in a year. In order to compete with other modes of transportation such as trucks, ships and barges, and aircraft, railroads are improving delivery times and on-time service while reducing shipping rates. As a result, businesses are expected to increasingly use railroads to carry their goods.

However, growth in the number of railroad transportation workers will generally be adversely affected by innovations such as larger, faster, more fuel-efficient trains and computerized classification yards that make it possible to move freight more economically. Computers are used to keep track of freight cars, match empty cars with the closest loads, and dispatch trains. Computer-assisted devices alert engineers to train malfunctions and new work rules have become widespread, allowing trains to operate with two- or three-person crews instead of the traditional five-person crews.

Employment of locomotive and yard engineers should grow as the industry expands and more trains are in operation, and because they will be less affected by technological changes and reductions in crew size.

Subway and streetcar operator employment is expected to grow as metropolitan areas build new rail systems and add new lines to existing systems. State and local governments support new construction because population growth in metropolitan areas has increased automobile traffic, making streets and highways more congested. Improved rail systems offer an alternative to automobile transportation that can reduce road congestion and, by reducing automobile use, contribute to government-mandated improvements in air quality.

SALARIES

According to the National Railroad Labor Conference (NRLC) in early 1997, the annual earnings for engineers ranged from an average of $52,903 for yard-freight engineers, to $65,374 for passenger engineers.

For conductors, earnings ranged from an average of $48,991 for yard-freight conductors, up to $62,169 for local-freight conductors.

The NRLC reports that brake operators averaged from $41,968 for yard-freight operators, up to $54,448 for local-freight operators.

According to mid-1997 American Public Transit Association data, hourly earnings of operators for commuter rail averaged $21.44; operators for heavy rail $18.70; and operators for light rail, $17.04. Wages generally varied from about $5 to $7 per hour in either direction on the high and low end.

Most rail transportation employees in yards work forty hours a week and receive extra pay for overtime. Most railroad workers in road service are paid according to miles traveled or hours worked, whichever leads to higher earnings. Full-time employees have steadier work, more regular hours, and higher earnings than those assigned to the extra board.

Most railroad transportation workers are members of unions. Many different railroad unions represent various crafts on the railroads. Most railroad engineers are members of the Brotherhood of Locomotive Engineers, while most other railroad trans`portation workers are members of the United Transportation Union.

Many subway operators are members of the Amalgamated Transit Union, while others belong to the Transport Workers Union of North America.

RELATED FIELDS

Railroad transportation workers deliver travelers and freight to destinations throughout the nation. Other workers performing similar duties include bus and truck drivers.

INTERVIEW
Steve Nichols
Terminal Superintendent

Steve Nichols started working for Norfolk Southern Railway Company in 1973 as a brakeman in Selma, Alabama. He is now a terminal superintendent in Birmingham, Alabama.

How Steve Nichols Got Started

"I grew up in a small town and there were few opportunities. The railroad has always been known for having a good salary and great benefits. Family and friends steered me toward the railroad. But at the time I was twenty years old and their hiring practice was 'must be over twenty-one.' Then they changed that rule and I was probably the first one in the door applying for a job.

"Most of my training was on the job and some at off-property schools such as Virginia Tech in Blacksburg, Virginia. The training was for management skills and transporting hazardous materials. I also participated in various seminars and courses through the years in alcohol and drug addiction, how to recognize it in the workplace, and operating and safety rules with yearly exams.

"To get started on the job I first had to take a mandatory test. This is where you are tested for consistency. The railroad wants someone who is sure of themselves and the decisions they make . . . not easily changing their mind. I was also tested for math and word usage and of course, the all important 'common sense' test.

"The next step was the interview. Here, they wanted to see how I handled myself with questions such as, 'Why does the railroad need me . . . what can I offer to the railroad?' Basically, this was to see the stability of the applicant.

"Once I was hired, I was trained on the job for six weeks. This has changed. Now you are trained for six months. This was the time to make sure I was capable of doing the job. It is a very physical job. After the six weeks, I established my seniority and was placed on a ninety-day probation period. This was to see if I would stay in place for calls. When you are hired by the railroad, you must provide a phone number where you can be reached. When you finish your day's work, you are entitled to an eight-hour rest. After eight hours, the railroad can call you for another job. You must be at the number you provide. If you are going somewhere other than home, you simply give the call office the new number, but they have to have a number.

"I started as a switchman on the extra board . . . on call. I was promoted in 1980 to a Terminal Trainmaster's position and was transferred to New Orleans. In 1985 I was promoted to Assistant Terminal Superintendent in Atlanta, Georgia. In 1986 I was promoted to Terminal Superintendent in New Orleans. In 1987 I was promoted to Terminal Superintendent in Macon, Georgia. In 1996 I was promoted to General Superintendent of Terminal Operations and Planning. In 1997 I was promoted to Terminal Superintendent in Birmingham, Alabama, which is my current position. Each position has held a higher ranking job with more responsibility and more people for whom I am responsible. I must say that the railroad has an excellent moving package for its employees."

What the Job's Really Like

"As a superintendent of a large terminal, I am in the office by six each morning. I always talk to the Trainmaster on duty around four-thirty every morning to get a rundown on the state of the terminal, what kind of problems we might have, what problems we've had in the last twenty-four hours, with detailed descriptions of any delays to trains, any derailments, and any plans for calling extras if business levels dictate. I have to know everything on my terminal. If I have problems in moving trains, that will ultimately give problems to the yards down the rail—a chain reaction. If Atlanta has a problem, Birmingham will, and then Chattanooga will, and so on.

"I am also responsible for overseeing the humping of some 1,600 to 2,000 cars a day, of pulling them out of the class yard, and building trains to depart. We run, on any given day some sixty trains in and out of the terminal.

"I am normally in the tower for two to three hours on a typical day (which means I am out of my office). I spend a couple of hours in the yard, making efficiency rule checks and safety audits. I do this a couple of times a week. Norfolk Southern is very safety conscious.

"Every day I have about two to three hours of paperwork. Each day, typically, I attend meetings, meet customers, and end up back in the tower for a couple of hours.

"It is always very, very hectic, but very interesting, however. I get to talk to all the other railroads and their superintendents around Birmingham about their operations.

"The atmosphere around the office and the terminal appears to me to be getting more and more like a safety team working together. It has been growing that way for many years. All of the other railroads are fighting hard to be number one in safety and knock Norfolk Southern out of first place. We have been number one as the safest railroad of all class-one railroads for nine years, going on ten. That is a goal achieved. We continue to be successful because we continue to work hard putting safety first. It is our number one priority, but with that comes a lot of pressure. There are a lot of details, details that have to be paid attention to, such as federal reporting of injuries on the railroad. You could lose a safety award from something as simple as an employee getting a bee sting. The public normally hears only about railroad accidents that are major.

"I normally leave the office between 5:00 and 6:00 P.M. Once home, I do spend a lot of time on the computer, looking at the different programs that NS has for us to use that makes it easier for us to be home but still working. We are becoming more and more automated and sophisticated.

"I am essentially on call twenty-four hours and I am readily available by beeper and phone at all times. Rarely, do I have a night that my phone doesn't ring. I am notified immediately of derailments or personal injuries. If an employee calls in sick or just doesn't show, I have to know. I have an assistant who splits the twenty-four hour clock with me. We alternate weekends off.

"My particular position with the company entitles me to five week's vacation, but the scheduling can interfere with weekends off. Sometimes I might work three weeks without any time off when my assistant is off on vacation. The long hours and the time away from home can be hard to deal with.

"But I don't know what I would be doing if I didn't work for the railroad and work these long hours. I enjoy my vacations, but after a week of being off, I'm usually looking forward to getting back."

Expert Advice

"Get a college education. You should strive to come up through the ranks. I think you will learn more about the railroad after a few years of experience. You will gain a lot, which will help you in future positions. An education in transportation and/or engineering is a plus, especially at the management level.

"You'll need lots of energy and patience. Also, you must be very safety conscious. At every hiring session, it is made clear from the beginning that you will work in all kinds of weather—heat, cold, storms, ice, snow—and holidays, and nights.

"Norfolk Southern's Personnel Department travels over the Norfolk Southern system, testing and interviewing prospective new hires for all departments and positions. Our personnel people do all the hiring for all departments and all levels in that department.

"We have a toll-free job line number that prospective employees can call for hiring sessions. It is updated each Friday. (The number is available through 800 directory assistance.)

"All new hires need to know we work on a seniority system. As a new hire you start at the bottom of the seniority roster. The only position that a new hire can hold is the extra board . . . meaning you are on call for the regular employees' off time. This means the senior employee probably will be taking off weekends and holidays.

"As a new employee, you will have to be available and reachable. There are a lot of rules, all for the safety of the employee. You must be willing to study, to learn, and abide by these rules.

"The benefits of the railroad are, in my opinion, the best. A great salary, great insurance, and a great opportunity for career advancement. I wouldn't want to be working anywhere else."

FOR MORE INFORMATION

To obtain information on employment opportunities for railroad transportation workers, contact the employment offices of the various railroads and rail transit systems, or state employment service offices.

For general information about career opportunities in passenger transportation, contact:

American Public Transit Association
1201 New York Avenue NW, Suite 400
Washington, DC 20005

General information on rail transportation occupations and career opportunities as a locomotive engineer is available from:

Brotherhood of Locomotive Engineers
1370 Ontario Avenue
Cleveland, OH 44113-1702

Association of American Railroads
50 F Street NW
Washington, DC 20001

For information on certification and training programs, contact:

Johnson County Community College
National Association of Railroad Sciences
12345 College Boulevard
Overland Park, KS 66210

CHAPTER 8 Travel Agents

EDUCATION
A.A. preferred

$$$ SALARY/EARNINGS
$16,000 to $33,000

OVERVIEW

Out of all the industries worldwide, travel and tourism continue to grow at an astounding rate. In fact, according to the Travel Works for America Council, it is the second largest employer in the United States (the first being health services). Nearly everyone tries to take at least one vacation every year, and many people travel frequently on business. Some travel for education or for that special honeymoon or anniversary trip.

At one time or another, most travelers seek out the services of a travel agent to help with all the details of a trip. This means that jobs for travel agents will continue to grow. Travel agents learn about all the different destinations, modes of transportation, hotels, resorts, and cruises, then work to match their customers' needs with the services travel providers offer.

Travel agents generally work in an office and deal with customers in person or over the phone. They plot itineraries, make airline and hotel reservations, book passage on cruise ships, or arrange for car rentals.

But first of all, they listen to the needs of their customers, then try to develop the best package for each person. They work with affluent, sophisticated travelers, or first-timers such as students trying to save money and travel on a budget. They could book a simple, round-trip air ticket for a person traveling alone, or handle arrangements for hundreds of people traveling to attend a convention or conference.

Some travel agents are generalists; they handle any or all situations. Others specialize in a particular area such as cruise ships or corporate travel.

Travel agents gather information from different sources. They use computer databases, attend trade shows, and read trade magazines. They also visit resorts or locations to get first-hand knowledge about a destination.

They have to keep up with rapidly changing fares and rates, and they have to know who offers the best packages and service. Their most important concern is the satisfaction of their client.

Most travel agents are offered "fam" trips to help familiarize them with a particular cruise line, safari adventure, exclusive resort, or ecological tour. These trips are offered free to the travel agent so they can "test-drive" a destination before suggesting it to their customers. Travel providers understand that a travel agent is more likely to sell what he or she knows and has enjoyed. Travel agents also receive discounted travel on other business trips, as well as on their own vacations.

The downside, however, according to many travel agents, is that they seldom have enough free time to do all the traveling they would like. They are often tied to their desks, especially during peak travel periods such as the summer or important busy holidays.

And the work can be frustrating at times. Customers might not always know what they want, or their plans can change, and as a result, the travel agent might have to cancel or reroute destinations that had already been set.

TRAINING

A four-year college degree is not necessary to become a travel agent. It can be helpful, however, and shows commitment and discipline. Most travel agents study for at least two years and earn an associate's degree. Many community colleges, trade and vocational schools offer good programs in travel and tourism or hospitality management.

Some travel agencies are willing to hire inexperienced applicants and provide them with their own training.

For a list of schools offering certified programs, you can write to the American Society of Travel Agents or the Institute of Certified Travel Agents. (Their addresses are listed at the end of this chapter.)

JOB OUTLOOK

Employment of travel agents is expected to grow faster than the average for all occupations through 2006. Many job openings will arise as new agencies open and existing agencies expand, but most openings will occur as experienced agents transfer to other occupations or leave the labor force.

Spending on travel is expected to increase significantly over the next decade. With rising household incomes, smaller families, and an increasing number of older people who are more likely to travel, more people are expected to travel on vacation— and to do so more frequently—than in the past. In fact, many people take more than one vacation a year. Business-related travel should also grow as business activity expands. Employment of managerial, professional, and sales workers—those who do most business travel—is projected to grow at least as fast as the average for all occupations. Charter flights and larger, more efficient planes have brought air transportation within the budgets of more people. The easing of government regulation of air fares and routes has fostered greater competition among airlines, resulting in more affordable service. In addition, American travel agents organize tours for the growing number of foreign visitors. Also, travel agents are often able to offer various travel packages at a substantial discount. Although most travel agencies now have automated reservation systems, this has not weakened demand for travel agents.

Some developments, however, may reduce job opportunities for travel agents in the future. The Internet allows people to access travel information from their personal computers and make their own travel arrangements. Suppliers of travel services are increasingly able to make their services available through other means, such as electronic ticketing machines and remote ticket printers. Also, airline companies have put a cap on the amount of commissions they will pay to travel agencies. The full effect of these practices, though, has yet to be determined as many consumers prefer to use a professional travel agent to ensure reliability and save time and, in some cases, money.

The travel industry generally is sensitive to economic downturns and international political crises, when travel plans are likely to be deferred. Therefore, the number of job opportunities fluctuates.

SALARIES

Experience, sales ability, and the size and location of the agency determine the salary of a travel agent. According to a Louis Harris survey, conducted for *Travel Weekly*, 1996 median annual earnings of travel agents on straight salary with less than one year experience were $16,400; from one to three years, $20,400; from three to five years, $22,300; from five to ten years, $26,300; and more than ten years, $32,600.

Salaried agents usually have standard benefits, such as medical insurance coverage and paid vacations, that self-employed agents must provide for themselves. Among agencies, those focusing on corporate sales pay higher salaries and provide more extensive benefits, on average, than those who focus on leisure sales.

Earnings of travel agents who own their agencies depend mainly on commissions from airlines and other carriers, cruise lines, tour operators, and lodging places. Commissions for domestic travel arrangements, cruises, hotels, sightseeing tours, and car rentals are about 7 to 10 percent of the total sale; and for international travel, about 10 percent. They may also charge clients a service fee for the time and expense involved in planning a trip.

During the first year of business or while awaiting corporation approval, self-employed travel agents generally have low earnings. Their income usually is limited to commissions from hotels, cruises, and tour operators and to nominal fees for making complicated arrangements. Even established agents have lower profits during economic downturns.

When they travel for personal reasons, agents usually get reduced rates for transportation and accommodations.

RELATED FIELDS

Other workers with similar duties include secretaries, tour guides, airline reservation agents, and rental car agents.

INTERVIEW
Vivian Portela Buscher
Travel Agent

Vivian Portela Buscher started out as a ticket agent and in passenger services for the airlines, then moved to a well-known cruise line as a booking agent. It was a natural progression for her to become a travel agent specializing in cruise travel and she has worked for the same agency now since 1987.

How Vivian Portela Buscher Got Started

"It's easy for me to advise other people about travel because it's something I like to do. I specifically chose to be a travel agent because working with the airlines had become difficult. You had to wait a long time to gain seniority and to have a comfortable work schedule with Saturdays and Sundays off. Plus, with so many airlines going out of business, there are a lot of unemployed people in the industry. The airline I worked for folded ten years ago and I was happy to switch. I was looking for a job that would still be in the travel industry but that would be more secure and with normal hours.

"When I went to college I studied air carrier management and received a bachelor's degree in transportation management. My experience with the airlines and then with the cruise line also was important in preparing me. The rest I picked up through on-the-job training."

What the Job's Really Like

"I work Monday through Friday, and because our agency is open from 9:00 A.M. to 9:00 P.M., I get to choose my hours during the day. Most people prefer to work earlier hours, but I don't. I work from 10:30 A.M. to 7:00 P.M.

"Basically, what I do is this: people call me who have an interest in taking a cruise vacation and I find them the right cruise at the right price. I think of it more as a matching game rather than a selling situation. My office doesn't call anyone asking them to buy a cruise; everyone calls us.

"I enjoy traveling and it's nice to be able to talk about it all day long and to help people find the right travel experience. There's a great deal of satisfaction when someone calls me back and tells me that the cruise was exactly as I had described it and that it was the best vacation of his or her life.

"You also get to travel yourself, to sample all the cruises and be more informed about them. I've been to St. Thomas, San Juan, Nassau, Grand Cayman, Jamaica, St. Lucia, and St. Martin, to name just a few places.

"We also get to attend many luncheons, dinners, and other inaugural activities to view the new ships.

"It's an office with a very high call volume. And there is always a lot of new information to learn, a lot of intensive studying you have to do to acquire all the product knowledge about all the different cruise lines and packages."

Expert Advice

"I think it's important to go to college and to get as much training as you can, and then to apply to work for an agency where you can get experience. Even if you get experience without going to school, it's very competitive. Sometimes the person with the most education will get the job over someone with equal experience."

INTERVIEW
Mary Fallon Miller
Travel Agent

Mary Fallon Miller started her career as a travel agent in 1986 when she opened her own agency. In partnership with a relative, she first focused on bus tours, transporting groups to see special events in her area. She later moved on to specialize in cruise travel.

How Mary Fallon Miller Got Started

"At the age of seven I sailed across the Atlantic on the S.S. *France,* and then, later, as a young woman, I accompanied my mother throughout Europe and South America. I fell in love with the glamour and excitement of travel. It gets in your blood; I have a real fascination for other cultures and languages. I realized that a career as a travel agent would allow me to pursue my dream to see more of the world."

What the Job's Really Like

"When you're just starting out, you're tied to the office and the computer a lot, but a newcomer would get to take at least one week a year, more once you've gained some seniority. The owners of a travel agency get to go on more 'fam' trips, but if someone just starting out is seen as a productive member of the business, helping to build it, he or she would get more opportunities. You'll be the one they send on the 'Cruise-a-Thon' or to the ski shows, and then you'll become your agency's representative.

"Beginners would probably start working side-by-side with someone more experienced in the agency. They might be placed in a specific department handling, for example, European travel, or cruises, or car rental and air fares. Much of their time will be spent coordinating and arranging details.

"It can be tricky keeping all the details accurate and being able to deal with what we call 'grumps and whiners.' These are the people who get very nervous about their travel arrangements and complain all the time. They can make your life miserable. But you have to be able to be compassionate—find out *why* they're so concerned. Maybe they had a bad experience in the past. You have to try to know as much about your client as possible.

"And there are times when things go wrong. There could be a snow-in at an airport and people miss their connections or someone in the family dies and they have to cancel their whole cruise reservation at the last minute. You have to be professional and flexible and you have to be on the ball all the time.

"It's a demanding job, but it's satisfying. People come back and say, 'I can't believe you knew exactly what I wanted. That's the best vacation I've ever had. And I'm telling all my friends.' You start getting more and more customers coming in and they ask for you by name. That feels really good. You're making a dream come true, and in a way, that's what you're doing—selling dreams."

Expert Advice

"Read *Time, Newsweek,* and your local newspaper. Try to stay in touch with the world. Listen to National Public Radio or watch the travel channel on television.

"Don't be afraid of learning the computer, studying languages, and participating in a language club or taking advantage of a foreign exchange program. I once lived in Poland for a summer.

"Most important, learn communication skills. And, at the beginning, when you're doing some of the drudgery work, it helps to remember that down the road you will receive discounts and free travel—you have something you are working toward. The hard work *will* pay off."

FOR MORE INFORMATION

American Society of Travel Agents
1101 King Street
Alexandria, VA 22314

Association of Retail Travel Agents
1745 Jefferson Davis Highway, Suite 300
Arlington, VA 22202

Institute of Certified Travel Agents
148 Linden Street
P.O. Box 56
Wellesley, MA 02181

About the Author

A full-time writer of career books, Blythe Camenson's main concern is helping job seekers make educated choices. She firmly believes that with enough information, readers can find long-term, satisfying careers. To that end, she researches traditional, as well as unusual occupations, talking to a variety of professionals about what their jobs are really like. In all of her books she includes first-hand accounts from people who can reveal what to expect in each occupation, the upsides as well as the down.

Camenson's interests range from history and photography to writing novels. She is also director of Fiction Writer's Connection, a membership organization providing support to new and published writers.

Camenson was educated in Boston, earning her B.A. in English and psychology from the University of Massachusetts and her M.Ed. in counseling from Northeastern University.

In addition to *On the Job: Real People Working in Transportation*, Blythe Camenson has written more than three dozen books for NTC/Contemporary Publishing Group.